Wheels Up

Mastering the Job Interview to Launch Your Career

The One Hour Handbook Series

by

Dr. Staci McIntosh

Published in the United States by Sensible Solutions
Henderson, Nevada

ISBN-13: 978-0-9992501-1-2
ISBN-10: 0-9992501-1-6

About the Author

Staci McIntosh has nearly 20 years of experience as a Human Resources executive in both public and private sectors. She has interviewed or coached over 1,000 individuals. Most have been just like you, wanting to perfect their skills for their next career move.

Staci writes her books with one goal: helping all people get the job they want. Through her brief, easy-to-read *One Hour Handbook Series,* she provides ambitious, hard-working people like you with useful tips you've probably never heard before. Staci knows her information will help you get your next job, because it's already worked for hundreds of others!

Staci entered the workforce as a teacher. She spent most of her career in the education field, eventually becoming an assistant superintendent and Chief Human Resources Officer. She then moved to the private sector. She is currently the Vice President of Human Resources for a popular casino resort on the Las Vegas Strip. Staci has a Bachelor's degree from Eastern Washington University, a Master's degree from Whitworth University, and an educational doctorate in leadership from Washington State University.

Staci lives with her husband Jim in Henderson, Nevada. Together they own Sensible Solutions, a consulting company devoted to providing practical resources for busy organizations and people. They enjoy eating great food on the Strip, binge-watching TV series, traveling, and spending time with Jim's teenage son Ben (an expert level Xbox One player) and Staci's daughter Kendall (a busy human resources professional).

To Barb
For your wisdom, for your guidance, and
For being a second mom to pretty much everyone

Table of Contents

Introduction

I n August of 2015, I decided to switch organizations and look for human resources work in another industry. Up to that point, I had spent my entire career working in education. Most of the time, I had considered myself a success. But professionally, the previous few years had been challenging. I was in a high-profile position, and people who had not even worked in human resources, or education, felt free to criticize my strategies. Once, after a particularly difficult day, I spent an entire Saturday in bed, binge-watching the Showtime series Dexter, just to cheer myself up.

On good days, I believed I was doing important work. I knew that even those who criticized were doing the best they could. I was strong, experienced, and knowledgeable. On bad days, I felt like the culture was wrong for me. I let myself believe I was responsible for situations that were well outside my scope of control.

As I look back on my experience, my beliefs about my good days and my beliefs about my bad days all contained some truth to them. In my heart, I knew it was time to look for another position, but for a long while I was afraid to make a move. So I continued to feel frustrated for not solving problems I felt I should be able to solve.

For me, it was a time filled with self-doubt. And it was getting worse. I didn't want to take risks. I was no longer playing to win. Instead, I was playing not to lose. I still loved human resources. I still loved many of the people I worked with. But I didn't love the feeling I felt when I was working.

Personally, however, I was lucky. I began dating Jim, I fell in love, and he became the man I would later marry. And guess where I found him? At work. In the "some things happen for a reason" category, this was a bright, happy example.

Because of our respective roles, we knew that when we got married, it would be disruptive to the organization. So, it made the most sense for me to be the one to leave. To do so, I relied on the strength and support of my husband-to-be.

Jim gave me the courage I needed to submit my intent to resign within the following year, giving our organization time for a transition. Before that, I had never quit one position before having another job offer to rely upon. It was an unsettling feeling, but I was optimistic about a new challenge.

Why am I sharing this experience? Because I want you to know that even experienced human resources professionals have self-doubt. I entered the interview process as nervous and as filled with insecurity as you might be right now. I had coached countless others about how to interview. I had myself interviewed hundreds of candidates. Now I was the one on the other side. The scary side. The side of self-doubt and questioning. The side of possible failure.

Because you may be feeling it too, I want you to know the fear I felt when I began thinking of interviews. I had to acknowledge my self-doubt. I had to feel it. I had to reckon with it. And ultimately, I had to push past it. Once I dealt with my self-imposed feelings of inadequacy, I aced interviews. Ultimately, I ended up with two job opportunities, both higher paying than the job I was unhappy in. The one I chose to pursue has provided me with the highest level of personal job satisfaction I have felt in a long time.

In this book, I will give you proven, practical, interview strategies. I devoted the first chapter to the feelings you might have. Those feelings can impact your interview performance without you realizing it. I share ways that you can face your fear of failure and your self-doubt.

Throughout the rest of the book, the specific interview techniques I provide will ensure the interview team judges you the best candidate for the job. I will explain how to anticipate questions. I will share with you common interview etiquette and what you should wear. I will provide you with tips to connect to the interview team, as well as how to handle some common interview formats. Finally, I will tell you what mistakes to avoid in order to let your personality, skills and experiences shine through to the interview team.

Chapter One

Being the Best at Being YOU

Most of us judge ourselves harshly. We worry about what other people think of our efforts, even if those people aren't part of our everyday lives. We wake up at 4:00a.m., our brains a never-ending audio loop of others' judgments. We imagine someone implied we are not smart enough, not experienced enough, not tall enough, not attractive enough, not hard-working enough, not well connected enough. We beat ourselves up over every mistake, wishing like hell we had known better and done more. We can't help but return on occasion to how we felt as an insecure seventh grader worried about where everyone else was sitting in the cafeteria.

These thoughts make us doubt our ability to do anything outside of our comfort zone. It's easy for the angst to hold us back from seeking and obtaining career advancement. In this chapter, I'm going to explain the hidden ways insecurity negatively impacts the success of your interview. Then I am going to provide you with precise strategies you can use to overcome it and impress the interview team with your confidence.

Insecurity and Impressions

If you don't work to overcome your fears, your insecurity becomes very apparent in interview situations. In candidates' examples, in their tone of voice, in the very way they position their bodies, self-doubt becomes evident. Regardless of the words you use, what you are feeling has an impact on the interview panel. Imagine a customer service agent who smiles nicely and says all the right things, but who you know thinks that customer is a pain in the ass. That is how powerful your unstated feelings are, relative to how you answer the question.

There are common ways people broadcast their own insecurity. The most obvious are the traditional behaviors demonstrated by people lacking confidence. They hunch over slightly, almost shrinking into the room. Their tone of voice is quiet and sometimes even tremulous. They use examples filled with words which hide their talents. They say, *The team had to communicate with many other departments* instead of saying *I coached my team to gather other department's input, and I made sure they understood strategies about how to truly listen to incorporate diverse ideas.* They stumble over their words and frequently get lost in questions. It becomes apparent that with every sentence they speak, they also have a running dialogue in their head judging themselves on their answer.

At the other end of the spectrum, some candidates work overly hard to hide their insecurity. They overcompensate by seeming arrogant in their answers. They clearly demonstrate a reliance on positional power. Their examples are replete with indicators that they order people around, disregard what their colleagues have to say, and don't listen to feedback. Even when the sentences seem standard, the interviewer nevertheless gets a "me first" vibe from the candidate's demeanor and the language he uses.

One of the most insidious ways a candidate's insecurity comes out in an interview is through perfectionism. The sad part is that it's obvious the candidate has prepared valiantly beforehand. The problem becomes that the candidate is obsessively focused on giving the exact right answer, in the exact format, with the exact tone he or she practiced. When the candidate is working that hard at being perfect, the interview comes across as mechanical at best.

At worst, the candidate makes robotic mistakes. He begins to answer a question. In his head he thinks he made a mistake, even if the interview team didn't realize it. He doesn't keep talking to try to get back on track. He just stops. Blank stare. Panicked look. Like a robot whose batteries died.

If you work hard to do well and you take time to practice, that is not perfectionism. Perfectionism is when you tell yourself that if everything doesn't go *exactly* as planned, *you* are a bad person. When plans get disrupted, do you get angry, have a meltdown, or yell at your partner? In essence, without even trying, you will show those strong emotions in an interview if you use perfectionism to fight insecurity. It's hard to seem confident in an interview if you hate yourself when you make a mistake.

Confidence and Presence

The strategies I am going to provide you in this chapter changed the way I prepared for my own interviews. These strategies also had a dramatic impact on how I approached any situation where I felt nervous, vulnerable, and fearful of fitting in or looking like a failure.

There are five books I rely upon to help me teach confidence when I provide career coaching to others. The first book is *Presence: Bringing Your Boldest Self to Your Biggest Challenges* by Amy Cuddy. Three of the books are by Brene Brown. The three books can be read as a series, but each book stands alone and can be read by itself. The first one written is *The Gifts of Imperfection: Let Go of Who You Think You're Supposed to Be and Embrace Who You Are.* The second one is *Daring Greatly: How the Courage to Be Vulnerable Transforms the Way We Live, Love, Parent, and Lead.* The third book is *Rising Strong: The Reckoning. The Rumble. The Revolution.* I discovered Brene's third book first, intrigued by her explanation on the book cover, as follows: *If we are brave enough, often enough, we will fail. This is a book about what it takes to get back up.* The fifth book is *Love Yourself Like Your Life Depends On It* by Kamal Ravikant. It's a short but powerful book that will take you less than an hour to read.

This chapter relies heavily upon the advice provided in these five books. I've summarized the parts that are most important, but all authors write in accessible, easy to understand language. They give helpful advice, and they tell of their own struggles with self-worth. The stories they share about themselves and others are inspirational and entertaining. If you don't like to read, I suggest watching these authors on YouTube or listening to their books in audio version while driving. I promise you won't be disappointed.

I've summarized the information into nine key strategies. These strategies will enhance your confidence and presence when answering questions. If you make mistakes, if you forget a question, even if you spill water all over the table, these actions will help you maintain a relaxed, positive feeling and confident outward demeanor. How you feel about yourself will translate to how the interview team feels about you.

Strategy #1: Reckon with the Past

If you are going into an interview having had a difficult career experience, you have to wrestle with it before you can do anything else. Think of it like a paper cut. First, it hurts like hell. Then you sort of get used to the stinging and you don't notice it as much. You ignore it. But then it becomes infected. You still notice it, but you continue to ignore it because you think, geez it's only a paper cut. Why does it still bother me? But it does, and it's not getting better. Ultimately, you have to re-examine the cut, and you'll probably put some medicine on it, but it feels worse before it gets better again. The same is true for a negative career experience. I call it PTJD--Post Traumatic Job Disorder.

If you don't address your feelings, those negative thoughts will stay there. They will lurk in the recesses of your mind. In your interview, your feelings will come out through a sarcastic comment, a negative example, or even a mean look you get when talking about your previous boss. How do you deal with PTJD?

The most important thing you need to do is bring it to the surface. Talk about your emotions to a friend, or write down your feelings. Identify what you think you are feeling, for example, *I feel ashamed I didn't do better. I feel hurt that I wasn't recognized. I am afraid no other employer will hire me. I feel pissed because it wasn't fair.*

Let yourself go into detail about every event that contributed to your current state of mind. As Brene Brown says, "The good news is that in our reckoning we don't have to pinpoint the emotion accurately--we just need to recognize that we're feeling something...This sounds pretty easy, but you'd be surprised how many of us never recognize our emotions and feelings--we off-load instead. Rather than saying *I failed and it feels so crappy,* we move to *I am a failure.* We act out and shut down rather than reaching out."

Once you've identified you own crappy feelings, close your eyes. Imagine yourself placing all your negative feelings in a box. Think of each of them as a bright sign with that specific word on it. Close the box tight. In your mind, take the box to the ocean and let it be taken out to sea. Feel the relief having those negative emotions washed away from you as you relax on the sand.

For those of you who like a more literal approach, write down every nasty, mean, unfair, profane description you want to about your experience. Write down the horrible feelings you felt. Write five fake emails to five people who you are particularly pissed at. Then take the pieces of paper into your backyard, and burn them. Feel your hurt and shame burn up and then dissipate into nothing, just like the smoke from the fire.

Strategy #2: Replace the Post Traumatic Job Disorder Feeling

Replace your negative feelings with new feeling patterns. Once you've imagined your negative thoughts leaving you, replace them with positive thoughts. Create a picture in your head of you doing outstanding work at a new job. Add to the picture the helpful insights you learned from your past experiences, both positive and negative. In the picture you are happy, working hard, and using all you've learned.

Now imagine you are in the audience at a movie, and all you see is a new scene where you are doing great. Put it on a mental loop. Once the scene starts to fade, you play it again. Play that scene all the time, not just when you're feeling self-doubt.

In his book *Love Yourself Like Your Life Depends On It*, Kamal Ravikant states, "Imagine a thought loop as this: a pathway laid down by constant use. Like a groove in rock created by water. Enough time, enough intensity, and you've got a river...a focused mental loop is the solution. Add emotional intensity if you can--it deepens the groove faster than anything...Whether you believe it or not doesn't matter, just focus on this one thought, *I love myself*. Make it your truth. The goal here is to create a groove deeper than the ones laid down over the years--the ones that create disempowering feelings...What you're creating is a new groove so deep, so powerful, that your thoughts will automatically flow down this one."

Strategy #3: Practice Positive Self-Talk

Speak lovingly to yourself, give yourself compliments, and do it out loud. I know it sounds silly. But some scientists believe that when you speak out loud this way, you re-program the pathways of your brain. Then, you begin to really believe what you are saying. When you're in your car or walking around your house alone, try saying some version of *I love myself* over and over. Say it like you mean it. Say it like you're saying *I love you* to someone else. Try other phrases like, *You are so smart! You're going to rock that interview!*

Say it with the enthusiasm you would say it with when encouraging your best friend. Kamal Ravikant says, "When we love ourselves, we naturally shine, we are naturally beautiful. And that draws others to us. Before we know it, they're loving us and it's up to us to choose who to share our love with. Beautiful irony. Fall in love with yourself. Let your love express itself and the world will beat a path to your door to fall in love with you."

Strategy #4: "Fake it until you become it."--Amy Cuddy

The work of Amy Cuddy asserts that how we behave impacts how we feel about ourselves. Amy's research shows that if I am smiling, the expression on my face makes *me* feel happy. In turn, the interviewers feel I'm authentic, not just smiling because I think I'm supposed to. If you're thinking to yourself *I'm nervous*, begin pretending you are not. Walk around as if you're excited. Begin telling your friends and family how you are looking forward to telling the interview team about your experiences. Really believe it. Think it. Talk about it. Reframe the experience from *I'm nervously freaking out* to *I've got this!*

Strategy #5: Use Body Language to Trick Your Brain

Amy Cuddy says, "Your body language shapes who you are." An expansion to the fourth strategy, I recommend this all the time. It's simple, easy, and it's based on a large quantity of science. Research shows that certain "power poses" trick your brain into giving you that inner confidence you need to succeed.

When you do these power poses, your stress hormone (cortisol) goes down, and your confidence hormone (testosterone) goes up. When your core biology gives you that boost of confidence, you feel calmer. The nasty little feelings of self-doubt recede, and as a result, your true self shines brightly to the interview team.

All power poses contain some version of an open stance with arms and legs uncrossed and open as well. Your chin is up, your posture is good. You take up more space, a phenomenon seen in the wild when the largest mammals among the tribe are usually the leaders. I first recommend power posing the day before the interview. Stand in front of a mirror. Pretend there is a person in front of you and practice saying hello maintaining an open stance. Practice shaking that person's hand with your legs slightly apart and your other arm hanging away from your body. Avoid the handshake method where you hunch over, almost looking up, putting your hands in front of you and meekly extending one hand to the other person.

If you search "Power Poses" on the internet, you can find a variety of them. There is the victory pose, with hands up in a "V". There is the wonder woman pose, with legs spread and hands on your hips. There is a pose jokingly referred to as man spreading: lying back in a chair with your arms up, legs spread, and taking up as much space as you can. On their own, power poses can quite effectively deliver you a dose of (subconscious) confidence. If you pair power posing with thoughts of real power, enormous success, and true victory, power poses work even better.

Right before the interview, use the restroom and do some power posing paired with visions of yourself rocking the interview. While in the waiting room, stay off your phone. That hunched over texting posture has been proven to have the opposite effect of power posing--adding to your anxiety. Instead, sit up straight. Be sure your feet are aligned with your shoulders, not crossed beneath you. Keep your arms away from your body so that they are open as well. Lift your chin up a little bit higher than normal. Better yet, stand up. Put your shoulders back, lift your chin up, and imagine yourself doing the victory pose.

During the interview, keep your body language open, and your brain will believe you are the most powerful mammal in the room. This will allow your words to flow more easily, while at the same time connecting to the audience. If you can, keep your feet uncrossed under the table. Don't clasp your hands together. Instead, keep them flat on the table or steepled (fingers together, but palms still open). Keep your shoulders back and posture straight. It's not just that you will appear more confident to the interview team. You will truly feel more confident.

When I began giving this tip, candidates reported back that, even if they didn't get that specific job, they felt better, more confident, and relaxed. In other words, if they didn't get the job--

someone had to have been more qualified, and they had no regrets.

Strategy #6: Practice, Practice, Practice, Relax

If you read my book *Ready for Take-Off: Preparing for Interview Questions on Your Job Search Journey,* you've practiced answering questions out loud until you have your main points memorized. You may have spent hours preparing, perhaps over the course of several days, and you're tired. When you've reached that point, you need to stop. Don't keep yourself up all night cramming in more and more information.

The day before the interview, by 6:00pm, just stop. Eat dinner, watch TV and relax. Get a good night's sleep. In the morning, review your notes only once. Give your brain some time to integrate what you've been learning. Continuing to cram when the interview time is getting nearer is only going to stress you out. Do your power poses, visualize yourself nailing it, and then relax.

Strategy #7: Meditate, Pray, or Do Both

Use deep, cleansing breathing. Fill your mind with positive thoughts, bathed in light, showing you images of yourself doing an amazing job. Ask God, the Universe, or your preferred Life Force to help you answer the questions. Ask to feel proud of yourself after the interview.

It's important when praying or meditating not to focus on the outcome itself. Focus on how you will feel during and after the interview, regardless of the outcome. Use the phrases *Thy will be done* or *And so it is* to help yourself be at peace with whatever happens.

Strategy #8: Think Gratitude

You might be almost broke. You may have been through terrible experiences. You may have legitimate reasons to be sad, pissed off, or afraid. Even with all those thoughts being true, you can still be grateful for something. Make lists in your head of all the conditions in your life you are thankful for. At the very least, you can be thankful for not having it as bad as some people.

Do this as you're practicing for the interview. Do this also while you're waiting to interview. When your brain and heart are filled with gratitude as you go into the interview, your positivity is palpable. Then, you are more likely to impress the interview team.

Strategy #9: Separate Negative Thoughts From Reality

In the same way positive thoughts spill over onto how the interview team feels about you, negative thoughts do the same. Most negative thoughts, however, are simply a reaction to an event. The thought is not the reality.

For example, say the interview scheduler was abrupt when talking to you on the phone. She cut you off before you could ask any questions about the interview. Your negative thought is, *I'm obviously not the best candidate or she would have treated me better.* That thought is the reaction *you* are choosing. You could just as easily choose the thought, *It must be really busy working there because they have so many clients! That's great!*

Negative thoughts are not reality. They are only your opinion of an event. Realize that by switching your negative thoughts to positive ones, you are also improving the person you project to the interview team.

Take the Shortcut

1. Judging yourself harshly can prevent you from advancing your career and can negatively impact the impression you give to the interview team.

2. Being timid, overcompensating by being arrogant, ignoring negative feelings, and being a perfectionist are all unproductive behaviors which can prevent you from doing well in an interview.

3. Use specific strategies to ensure your confidence level is high when you are interviewing. When you are confident, it impacts your brain's ability to answer questions. Being confident also has a positive impact on how the interview team feels about you.

Chapter Two

Preparing for Interview Questions

In my book *Ready for Take-Off: Preparing for Interview Questions on Your Job Search Journey,* I go into great detail about how to prepare and practice for an interview. That book provides much more detail than this chapter. However, if you haven't read that book, in this chapter I have summarized that book's most important guidance. I will discuss doing research, anticipating questions, organizing your answers, and practicing out loud.

First, do some preliminary research. Find out what is important to that future employer by researching the company so that you know what type of person they like to hire. Read the job description thoroughly to ensure that you meet the qualifications for the position. Ensure you have at least some experience in each of the job responsibilities they have listed. Prepare by specifically identifying your past accomplishments. Then match your own accomplishments to the expectations on the job posting.

Next, anticipate what the interview will be like. Use the job description to create questions the interview panel might ask. Google the type of job and interview questions to get additional ideas for that specific job type. Look on job posting website forums to learn other questions this company might have asked prior candidates.

After you have anticipated questions, organize your answers. Outline each answer with a topic or broad statement followed by examples. Be sure to hit both broad and specific when outlining your answers. Use different examples for different questions.

Once you've outlined answers on paper, memorize the main points of your answers. Begin practicing them out loud. Practice until you have the answers memorized and can remember easily the examples you will provide for each topic. Finally, do a dress rehearsal by getting into your interview suit and having friends or family members ask you questions. Add in some appropriate humor. Include new or original thinking that other candidates might not mention.

The important thing for you to consider is that preparation is key to your success. Each interview question is much like an impromptu speech. You should prepare for the content as you would prepare for a particularly difficult test. You need to anticipate, study, memorize, and practice before you get to the interview. If you've never been taught how to fully practice for an interview, I strongly encourage you to download my book on this topic. If you already know how to prepare, then the next chapters will give you specific guidance for the actual interview itself.

Take the Shortcut

1. Use the job posting or job description to generate probable questions.

2. The internet, as well as books which give sample interview questions, are valuable resources to prepare for interview questions.

3. Anticipate questions that will be related to the job responsibilities. Also anticipate questions that will ask you about your personality traits or work style.

4. Organize your answers into a clear structure that will be easy for the interview team to understand.

5. Memorize your key points and practice your interview questions out loud until you can deliver the answer flawlessly.

Chapter Three

Interview Etiquette Secrets

There are great similarities between an interview and a formal social situation. Both require etiquette knowledge. Both have a specific set of protocols and expectations that aren't necessarily written down anywhere. For both, the etiquette required may vary from one place to another.

People who are new often do not understand the importance of adhering to the accepted etiquette. But when they don't, they are less likely to be accepted by the group. In an interview situation, failing to follow etiquette standards may lose you the job, even if you do well answering questions.

On the other hand, understanding and exhibiting the expected behaviors can help you connect with interviewers. By the end of this chapter, you will understand why you should arrive far earlier than the start time of the interview. You will know the importance of greeting everyone in a friendly and warm tone, without going overboard. Finally, you will know what to wear, and what not to wear, to the interview.

Arriving Early

I once worked for a superintendent who had a favorite saying about people being late to meetings. She said, "Better late than never, but better never late." I'm pretty sure she got the saying from her former boss, and it's a good mantra to follow. I have always been an on-time person. Still, she reinforced to me that being late to a meeting subtly tells everyone else that your time is more important than theirs. It is disrespectful to those around you.

The same is true for interviews. It goes without saying that being on time is an expectation of an interview. However, there are some people for whom being on time is a challenge. They arrive late for committee meetings. They arrive late for events. They are the last to rush in to their kid's basketball game. If you are late to a job interview, the panel will judge you as sloppy, maybe even lazy. They will have a negative impression of you no matter what you say or do.

I have had individuals arrive late to an interview for very understandable reasons. A traffic accident in front of them. Coffee spilling on their interview attire. Teenagers who failed to arrive home in the car needed to drive to the interview. As human resources professionals, we get it. However, no matter what the reason, you are going to be judged poorly.

For this reason alone, you need to plan to arrive far earlier than your interview start time. Fifteen minutes is never a good rule of thumb. The best rule of thumb is that however long it will take you to travel to your interview, plan on arriving that amount of time early. For example, arrive at least a half-hour prior to the start of the interview if your interview location is a half-hour drive away. If the interview will take you at least an hour to get to, then plan on arriving an hour early. If you are travelling by airplane to your interview, plan on arriving the night before.

Planning for this amount of time provides you plenty of cushion in case you encounter traffic or other delays. Even if you get into a minor car accident on the way to the interview, you will still have time to call Lyft or Uber to get you there. If you get halfway to your destination and spill coffee all over yourself, you have time to go back and change, or even stop to get a new outfit. (Tip: don't bring liquids other than water in the car to your interview).

Planning for this amount of time also gives you think time in the car before you actually go in. You can review your notes. You can practice your answers out loud. You can meditate. You can visualize yourself nailing the interview. You can imagine everyone smiling and loving you at the interview.

This also gives you time to find the actual location of the interview, if it's in a large complex or building. Once you get there, it gives you time to hit the restroom and do your power poses behind closed doors. Once you're in the general location of the interview, then you can arrive in the exact room or office twenty minutes early.

Your promptness will be recognized. Arriving in the room or office twenty minutes early will also give you potentially valuable information. You'll most likely be there when the previous interviewee leaves. You might know the person. You'll observe if one of the panelists walks the person all the way out the door. That way, you can mentally prepare for the interaction after the formal interview.

Greetings

No matter where you are in the interview phase, whether it's speaking with a scheduler, interacting with a recruiter, or waiting in the CEO's office for a final interview, you are in the interview. Do not make the mistake of appearing rude, disinterested, or dumb during informal interactions.

At all times, smile and speak warmly to any employee you encounter. Use a friendly, professional tone whether you are talking in person or corresponding via email. In all of my positions, I have had the great fortune of having excellent staff members working for me. Typically, they meet and interact with candidates long before I do. They always report back when an applicant exhibited behavior that was inappropriate for the situation.

Once a candidate for a high-level technology position called one of my application specialists for help. He couldn't understand the new on-line application, requested a paper one, and then sarcastically commented that our application wasn't more user-friendly. Needless to say, although he was already scheduled for an interview, he lost the job before he even arrived.

Ironically, he was actually correct. We ourselves knew it was time to upgrade our system, but we hadn't been allocated a budget to do so yet. No matter how difficult the on-line process was, that candidate looked dumb--more so because he was applying for a high-level technology position. And he was rude to the person trying to help him as well. The time to suggest changes to hiring processes you may not have found helpful is after you get the job, not before.

You should expect that how you greet and interact with support staff throughout the process will be noticed. It will be reported on as well, if it is outside the expected norm. People will judge you if you treat employees who are not in power positions differently from how you treat everyone else. If you are dismissive or rude, they will tell the boss.

Be sure that you smile and offer to shake the hand of everyone you meet along the way. Engage in conversation if you're in a waiting room and it seems appropriate. At the very least, give a friendly hello. But don't go overboard. Overly friendly behavior can have an impact as well.

Here is an example to illustrate the point. I was leading a panel of people interviewing for a principal position. One candidate, "John", was very enthusiastic. He came highly recommended and was from another organization. He gave a loud, boisterous hello to everyone he met. His emails about the interview details were filled with multiple exclamation points. When he came for the interview, he went out of his way to say hello to my assistant and gave her a gift. He was very likable.

The problem was, he was difficult to take seriously. Everything about him screamed *overeager* and we weren't sure if that was because he was desperate to be a principal, or that he was just a loud, smiling, and friendly person. He was loud during the interview. His presentation contained a lot of bright colors and photographs with him in them. To me, it felt like John believed everyone was his best friend. To my assistant, it felt creepy. To the people on the panel, it felt like he would not fit well into our somewhat conservative culture.

The best strategy is to be both friendly and warm. Warm can be an ambiguous term so I'm going to take the time to explain it here. Warm means smiling and initiating a hello. Warm means being authentic--being yourself, while being aware of interview etiquette norms. Warm means being relaxed and appearing confident, yet humble. If you want to see someone being warm on video, I suggest you watch a morning news host interviewing someone who isn't famous or who isn't a politician. Both national and local morning hosts, in my view, tend to be warm to non-famous people in order to make them feel comfortable. Watch what they do and then actively try to emulate their body language and speech.

I am always asked a question about shaking hands with everyone on a panel, if there are a lot of people. My suggestion is that you always assume you are going to walk around the table, smiling and greeting everyone on the interview panel. This shows respect for each individual and demonstrates confidence. It also allows you to make initial eye contact with everyone who will be gauging your performance. If you are a person who gets nervous and your palms sweat, use these strategies.

First, while you're getting ready at home, put clear, non-show anti-perspirant on your hands. Let it dry and then make sure there is no residue by slightly rubbing your hands on a tissue. While waiting at the location of the interview, do not hold your hands together. Instead, keep your hands with palms open while standing, or open on the arms of a chair if sitting. Using these strategies should help you avoid the sweaty palm problem.

Greeting each person you meet with a smile and a handshake will make a good impression on everyone who works at the organization. If you fail to do so, you run the risk of appearing too timid for the position, or even rude. Ensuring your greeting is friendly, confident, and warm adds to a positive impression that will increase your chances of getting a job.

Attire & Grooming

Most people will tell you to wear a suit, a shirt and tie, or a dress with jacket for an interview. I don't disagree with that advice. I do think there are more decisions to make about your attire than what most people realize. What you wear and your other personal grooming choices give the interview panel a first impression before you even say one word.

There is one overarching philosophy you need to follow. You don't want any part of your personal appearance to detract from what you're saying. You don't want the interviewers to be thinking about your very fashionable, yet very funky, shoes. You might think that wearing a novelty, cartoon tie makes you seem more approachable. Instead, the interviewer may consider *you* to be cartoonish.

A navy blue, black, or grey color palette is easy to find and usually something you'll wear in the future. Use bright colors only if appropriate for the job. Shine your shoes and cover your tattoos. You should appear clean, ironed, and well groomed. In essence, you're aiming for attire that is appropriate and which remains in the background relative to your words and thoughts.

One factor which should drive your decision is the type of job you're applying for. For most jobs, a suit, shirt and tie, or dress and jacket are all appropriate. However, what if you're applying to be a cocktail server? A suit or suit jacket is likely to make you seem too stuffy. A nice dress is probably best in those circumstances. Maybe you're applying for a fashion industry job. If that's the case, you will want to wear the most fashion-forward outfit you can find, and that may include funky shoes. If you're applying to be a plumber, mechanic, carpenter or other trades position, it might be more appropriate to wear nice slacks and a shirt, without a tie.

Interviewers tend to hire those who look like themselves. While you don't want to be the only one in the room without a tie, you usually don't want to be the only one in the room *with* a tie, either. That said, you're safer making the mistake of being more formal than the job requires, not less.

The next factor you'll want to consider is the interview format and set up. In many interviews, you will be sitting at a table with the interviewer or panelists also at the same table. In that case, women can feel comfortable wearing a skirt suit or a pantsuit.

However, for managerial roles, many times you'll meet the head of the department or CEO in his/her office. In those cases, the set up may be more informal. You might be sitting on a couch. If you're a woman and you think you're going into a more informal setting, wear a pantsuit instead. The last thing you want is to be distracted trying to keep your knees together perfectly so the interviewer can't see your Spanx.

You might also be participating in the "take a tour" format, described later in this book. If that's the case, it's best for women to wear low-heeled or even flat shoes with a pantsuit. Depending on the facility, men or women might also choose flat boots or shoes with more comfortable soles. Again, your goal is to wear clothes that don't detract from what you're saying. But you also need to wear attire that isn't likely to distract yourself, either. If the walking tour lasts an hour, and your shoes end up killing your feet, you're not going to be giving the most thoughtful answers.

The next piece of advice also applies to both men and women. Choose an outfit that fits you well, and have it dry cleaned or iron it yourself. Most people can't afford to get their outfits tailored. Thus, what you wear will probably be bought off the rack, or even borrowed from a friend. That is perfectly fine. Just be sure what you're wearing isn't too tight or too loose. You want to be certain it's not gapping in areas that inadvertently show your undergarments.

If you are overweight, underweight, very tall or very short, it's well worth it to buy clothes that fit your body type well or to have your clothes tailored. I have found that some individuals with body shapes outside the average drown in their clothes, buying outfits that are loose fitting and hang on their bodies. First impressions of these individuals include assumptions of sloppiness or a lack of confidence. When your body is swimming in your clothes, it's difficult for your personality to shine through.

Don't buy clothes that are too tight, either, even if you have ripped muscles or a perfect bikini body. Big or small, short or tall, make sure your clothes fit your body type. If you take the time to ensure your clothes fit you perfectly, you will feel more confident and you will look more polished. Most importantly, your visual appearance will not detract from your answers.

Personal grooming is also important. First, make sure your fingernails are clean and well groomed, of natural length, either nude without polish or polished in a French manicure. Any other colors can appear distracting, especially sparkling, black, blue and bright red. Individualize your nails once you get the job. In the interview, you don't want to risk having your nails be the focus of attention.

Next, ensure your hair isn't going to fall in your face. If you have long hair and you know it will stay back, and if you know you won't nervously play with it, feel free to wear it down. If there is any chance it might fall in your face, put it in a ponytail or pull it up.

If you're a man with long hair, I suggest keeping it back when interviewing with more conservative companies and cultures. Otherwise, if it looks good down and it's not in your face, you're fine leaving it down.

Another consideration is your facial grooming. Both women and men need to be sure that their eyebrows are waxed or otherwise neatly plucked. It may sound picky, but I interviewed one person who had an out-of-control "uni-brow" with hairs that stuck out horizontally. It was the very first thing the panelists commented on after the person left the room. It was distracting, and it made us wonder if his overall grooming would be poor if hired.

Men should trim their beards for interviews. It's safest to have it very neatly trimmed, but if you're dead set on wearing it long, then do so. Just make sure it's clean, combed, and not scraggly.

Women should pluck. Use a magnifying mirror and make sure you catch those stray hairs that seem to come out of nowhere. Do not wax your face right before an interview. If you want to do it, plan for waxing several days before. If you do it the day before or the morning of the interview, you could be left with splotchy red spots that look like acne.

In terms of scent, don't wear any except your deodorant. Many individuals have sensitivities to fragrance. Those who don't might still be distracted by a strong scent in a small, hot interviewing room.

Keep any make-up light. You want to look good. But you don't want to appear as if you're ready for a night on the town. Face makeup, light blush, mascara, light eye shadow and only a little bit of eyeliner is all you should use. This is no time to go for a smoky eye look unless your interview is for a job where you will (legally) be judged on your appearance, such as "model-hostess" or "model-server" positions.

Do not, under any circumstances, show cleavage. Check your top by bending over and looking at it from all angles. In warm climates especially, it seems like no one wants an extra layer. However, this is what camisoles are for. If you can see any part of your breast, put one on. Buy a good bra that fits you well, whether your breasts are large or small. Be sure it is thick enough to prevent any part from showing through.

My final piece of grooming advice is for both men and women. If your clothes show panty/underwear lines, or if your stomach hangs over the top of your pants, get some Spanx or other undergarments that pull you in and smooth you out. You are going to feel better knowing you have a clean-lined and professional look.

I now want to address the understandable questions from individuals who have visible scars, rosacea, psoriasis, or other physical characteristics over which they have no control, but which impact their appearance. My reassurance for you is this. Interview teams care far less about appearance issues that *cannot* be controlled than they care about appearance choices that *can* be controlled. Your appearance is not an issue compared to the guy who didn't take the time to iron out the fold lines in his Costco dress shirt.

What I find with individuals who have unique physical characteristics is that these can be a strength when paired with a confident, experienced, demeanor. It's up to you to determine if you want to address the physical characteristic or not. Sometimes it's better to give people information rather than having them wonder. If you want to say something, I usually suggest addressing it privately in advance of the interview, to the person in charge. You might say, *Hey, I don't want the interview team to be surprised, so I wanted to tell you this in advance. I do have some scars on my face that I received from a car crash. It's no big deal, and I'm fine now, and there is no pain that would impact my work. But I thought it would be good to tell you in advance so people aren't wondering about it when I interview. Thanks so much, I look forward to meeting you in person!*

It takes the highest level of character and confidence to overcome a physical trait outside the norm. When you come to the interview and demonstrate that confidence, it's a huge indicator of your ability to succeed. Adhere to the attire suggestions that you can implement, and you're going to really impress the interview team.

In summary, the appearance choices you are in control of are going to contribute to the impression you have on the interviewers, good or bad. Those who interview successfully know this. You could, understandably, make the decision that you don't want to work for an employer who won't allow you to be yourself when it comes to your attire choices. That is your choice. Just know that no matter what you decide, being aware of the choices you have is important. The key is that you know when you're making a decision.

I don't want you to make a mistake because no one gave you the information. My comments in this chapter can be unwritten rules to some people. I want you to be in the know. I want you to feel like you've made choices that will enhance, not detract from, your impression on the interview team.

Take the Shortcut

1. Interview etiquette includes the unwritten rules and ways of acting that can hurt or enhance your impression on the interview team.

2. Arrive at the interview location at a time equal to the travel time it will take you to get to the location. For example, if it takes you an hour to travel to the interview location, plan to arrive an hour in advance. This helps you to plan for any unforeseen circumstances and demonstrates respect to the interview team's time.

3. Greet everyone you meet with a friendly smile and handshake, and do not treat people who have positional power differently from those who do not.

4. Make sure no part of your attire or grooming has a chance to distract from the words you speak during the interview.

Chapter Four

Connecting to the Team

Some time ago, my husband Jim had an interview with a new organization. The interview was with a panel. None of them knew Jim personally, even though they had heard of his work through mutual connections. He was highly qualified for the job. Obviously, I had given him my best one-on-one interview coaching. He was prepared for the questions. He had multiple examples to share on a variety of potential topics. As his interview approached, I texted him, "Relax, and smile!"

When you first meet him, Jim has a serious demeanor. He is an observer in new situations, holding back and analyzing the landscape before jumping in to say something. I knew there was the possibility he would seem cold in the interview, preventing a connection to the team.

Luckily, Jim was selected to be a finalist for the next step. His main competition included a well-liked internal candidate and an external candidate described as extremely nice. Both had less experience than Jim, but we suspected they had connected more with the interview panel. I told him it was time for some intense Connection Coaching. He listened and got the job. Later, a colleague told him, "You did a good job and you were the most qualified on paper. But in the first interview, you seemed really quiet and stiff. Good thing you loosened up for the second one!"

Making a connection with the interviewers is very important to your success. Selection decisions are frequently based on the likability of the candidate, even if he/she has less experience than others. Creating an emotional connection with the interviewing team gives them a gut feeling, an intuitive sense, that you would be a great member of their team.

Lucky for you, there are specific strategies you can use to help others feel connected to you. In this chapter I will discuss how interviewing is like networking. I will then share how you can connect to interviewers by putting yourself in their shoes, by asking interesting questions, and by using sincere compliments.

Real Time Networking

An interview situation is like a high-stakes networking opportunity. People ask you about yourself, you talk, but at the same time you're also trying to make friends. You've probably met someone before who is very smart, but who nobody likes. Maybe the person seems cold, or distracted. You might think to yourself, *Wow, I could really learn something from her!* But your emotional side doesn't feel a connection and wouldn't want her as a member of the team.

After you've left the interview, you want people to believe that you can do the job well. Along with that, you want people to believe you would be a fun, friendly and pleasant member of the team. You might be thinking, *But wait, I'm an introvert! I can't be that outgoing!* Don't worry. Being an introvert does not mean you can't connect. In fact, I've seen many outgoing people who talk a lot, but they don't connect at all with people.

Sometimes introverts can be among the most effective at making connections with others, because they tend to listen better. I've coached introverts by giving them a few simple techniques when in networking situations. I find that they frequently become better than the extroverts. Introverts easily pay close attention when others speak, and hence their conversation partners feel valued.

In his book, *Everyone Communicates, Few Connect: What the Most Effective People Do Differently,* famous leadership expert John Maxwell states, "You will only be able to reach your potential--regardless of your profession or your chosen path--when you learn to connect with other people. Otherwise, you'll be like a nuclear power plant disconnected from the grid. You'll have incredible resources and potential, but you will never be able to put them to use."

In other words, you may have the best technical interview ever, providing lots of examples and experience. And yet you might still seem boring or stiff to the interview team. As you will see, all of the strategies in this chapter also apply to any networking situation. Use them to help you connect during the interview, but also use them to network with others long before you actually need to begin searching for a job.

Put Yourself in Their Shoes

The first strategy to connect is to put yourself in the mind of the interviewer. Imagine being on the other side of the table. Pay attention to each individual's body language and expression. If they are a jovial, loud group, imagine yourself simply joining them at a party. If they are a quiet, serious group, imagine that you're at a party and it's your job to get them excited or entertained.

Putting yourself in the mind of the interviewers allows you to empathize with their point of view. People want a team member who will understand them, who will fit in to their work culture and thought patterns. If during the interview one of the panelists thinks to herself, *That's just what I was thinking!* you have made a connection to that person.

If you're not psychic, you may be asking yourself how to figure out what the panelists are thinking. It's not as hard as you might anticipate. Imagine sitting in a room all day long, listening to others talk about themselves. You want to find that new team member who will get along great with everyone.

But it can get boring. It can get tiring. Sometimes you start to wish for anything or anyone to energize you. In addition, most people selected to be on interview panels are ambassadors for the organization. As a hiring manager, you don't want to put your most negative person on an interview panel. You want to put your generally positive, productive, and best team members in front of candidates. So, you're in front of busy professionals who may be tired, but who are among the organization's star players.

Imagine yourself on their side of the table. What would *you* want? First, demonstrate understanding for their situation. Make a comment such as any of the following:
I'm sure this is keeping you from your busy schedule today!
Thanks for taking the time to meet with me.
Uh-Oh. Looks like I'm the first interview after lunch. I'll try to keep it exciting so that the sugar low doesn't hit you.
It's at the end of your day, so I bet you're tired. Hopefully you saved the best for last! Thanks so much for meeting with me today. I know what the beginning of the week is like and it can be crazy coming off of the weekend.

These comments are positive and let the interview team know that you've been there. The comments give the team the impression that you are like them and that you understand how they are feeling. Finding a commonality is one of the best ways to connect with people. Weaving in common interests or background information will help as well.

For example, if someone on the team has a knee brace on, and you've also had knee surgery, you might say, *Hey, how are you healing? I went through that and it hurt for days!* If you happen to notice someone is wearing a tie with the new Las Vegas Golden Knights symbol on it, you could say, *Great tie, can't wait until their first season,* or even, *Great tie, I haven't paid attention to hockey before but I sure am going to do so now!*

If you're in a group of people from mixed departments, and you're used to working with those areas, you can comment on specific characteristics as well. For example, I was a candidate interviewing with a panel that contained a Chief Financial Officer. There was a question regarding collaboration among other departments. I jokingly said, "Even though Human Resources wants to spend money and Finance wants to save it, I can speak 'CFO'. I'm married to one." The comment got a good laugh from the team before I gave them a specific example from my work. For more strategies on how to find common characteristics of the team or organization you're interviewing with, check out *Ready for Take-Off: Preparing for Interview Questions on Your Job Search Journey,* my book on how to intensely prepare for interviews.

Humor is always a great way to connect. Your future coworkers want to be around someone who is happy. When you make light jokes or use humor, you show the team that you can loosen up and have fun with them. Early in my career, one of the highest compliments I received was from a colleague. I was interviewing for a position which had supervisory authority over him, and he had many years more experience than I did. He said, "The thing about Staci is, she takes the job seriously, but she doesn't take herself too seriously." That's the impression you want to leave with the interview team. You're a seriously hard worker, but you'll be a fun team member, too.

Ask Interesting Questions

Depending on the format, you may be prompted to ask questions at the end of the interview. If it's in a more informal setting, you may be expected to keep up an entire conversation by asking questions. No matter what the situation, be sure your questions are interesting. Make them questions that someone might have to think about, and avoid questions that can be answered with a simple yes or no.

For example, don't ask, *Do you like working here?* Instead, ask, *What's your favorite part of working here?* Or, *Tell me a time when you were really proud to work here.* Or, *What's the most fun thing you've done since working here?*

The questions you ask should also be positive in nature. There is a widely known psychology trick which helps you connect with other people. When you want to leave a good impression, and you only have the chance to ask a few questions, ask the committee to comment on something that will evoke a positive feeling. While they are telling you the event, that warm feeling they are experiencing will be connected to you. Hence, you will be seen as warm.

For the same reason, I strongly recommend against asking questions such as, *What's the most challenging aspect of working here?* Those questions force the organization's high-fliers to say something negative about a place they most likely love working at. In informal situations, there will be a lot of back and forth questions that aren't pre-scripted. Thus, you can usually get away with asking a few questions about strategic challenges, but only in the context of how you could contribute.

To remain positive, ask questions about the best parts of working there, the history of the organization, personal experiences working for the company, and even some technical questions. If you do ask about challenges, focus on business challenges. Avoid sounding like you are seeking negative attributes of the organization.

In addition, always stay away from pay, benefits, and selection process questions. You can ask selection process questions later in an email follow up, and you don't need to worry about pay and benefits until you're offered the job. Those questions are a waste of your precious interview time.

Use the end of the interview to ask interesting questions that will show you have researched the company in some regard. There may be a new company initiative, a recent news story, or something you've observed or heard while researching the company. Use that information to frame a question at the end of the interview. Make sure it's the type of question that will make the interview team think, but isn't so difficult that it makes you sound like a pretentious know-it-all.

Other good questions are along the lines of, *What are some of the benefits you've seen so far regarding (x) initiative? Or, I saw on the news that your company (did something great). What were some of the strategies you used to accomplish that goal?* If you've done your research on the company or the interview team, you might find blogs, articles, strategic planning documents, or other publications authored by the company or one of the members of the interview panel. Asking a question about the content of one of those publications helps the interview team know that you've taken the time to read their information.

I was once being interviewed by the newly appointed CEO of an organization. In his first six months on the job, he had published a document laying out his observations, initiatives, and strategies which would become the focal points of his work over the upcoming year. During the interview, the CEO asked if I had seen the document. Thank goodness, I had read it. He asked, "So, tell me what's missing?" I was able to speak confidently about the document during the interview.

Since he was obviously proud of his plan, I also used the time at the end of the interview to ask more probing questions about it. Later, I found out that the competitors for that job, two internal candidates, had not even read the document. Taking the time to understand the company and the panelists helps you answer, and ask, interesting questions. It helps you have authentic dialogue with the team. That in turn helps you connect to them, making a good impression.

Give Sincere Compliments

One of the best ways to connect with people in any situation is to give a compliment. If you've ever come across someone who looks disengaged or even upset, you know the reaction of a wide smile when you pay the person a compliment. The same is true for the people on the interview team. To have the desired effect, however, you first need to ensure that the compliment is sincere and authentic. Upon meeting the team, if you shake hands and give every single person a compliment, it's going to sound weird and slightly creepy.

The key is for you to work in more subtle compliments throughout your interview. Upon meeting the person who takes you into the interview room, you might say, *What a great tie!* if the person is wearing a color or pattern that you're particularly fond of. After saying your hellos to the interview panel, you might comment on the organization's friendliness, saying, *Everyone has been so nice to me here, what great customer service!* You could comment on a positive interaction with an employee who gave you directions. When you compliment members of the group or the whole organization, everyone feels good about what you said.

I was once leading an interview panel that was fairly talkative. As I walked into the room with the candidate, the team was laughing at something one of them had said prior to our arrival. I jokingly told the candidate, "Sorry, this bunch is hard to control!" Immediately, the candidate replied, "That's totally fine. It's so great that you all can have fun together. I think it's important to have that environment, and besides, it's already making me feel more relaxed." With that one comment, the candidate had managed to connect with the whole team.

While during the interview, you can give other compliments. If the person identified as the lead sales manager asks a question such as *What strategies do you use when you think you're about to lose a sale?* you could say, *I know you're asking the question, but I can tell that's never happened to you, right?* Then smile widely and laugh. Using humor while delivering a sincere compliment takes away the appearance that you are sucking up to any one individual.

Another strategy you might use is at the end of the interview. When asked what questions you have, you can compliment the team. You can say, *First I'd like to thank you so much for the opportunity to interview today. I can tell by the questions that you are really committed to finding the right match for this job. I hope I'm it, but if not, you asked some great questions to help us get to know each other. Also you were very welcoming, and I appreciate it. I do have a few questions, and they are...*

A final word about compliments. Make sure that the compliment applies to the person, but do so without giving the appearance of flirting. Also, make sure it's something unique that others might not notice or comment on. Telling a beautiful woman who has enormously blue eyes, *Wow, your eyes are so beautiful* is a little obvious and may seem flirtatious. Instead, try saying something like, *I so appreciate your assistant giving me perfect directions, she was great!* Focusing on the individual's leadership instead of personal appearance is always a safer approach.

Take the Shortcut

1. Imagine yourself as the interviewer to exhibit genuine empathy that lets the panel know you understand how they are feeling.

2. Ask interesting questions throughout the process to demonstrate a desire to know more. Also ask questions which generate happy responses that are likely to enhance the team's positive perception of you.

3. Use sincere compliments to show the interview panel that you appreciate them and to further influence their regard for you as a team member.

Chapter Five

Addressing Sticky Situations

During the interview, you may be faced with questions or problems you're not sure how to handle. You can, and should, prepare to address questions about any previous employment issues. How to handle the answers, however, can be complex depending on the situation.

There are other issues that you can't anticipate. And yet they do happen. Accidents. Interruptions. You name it, and pretty much I've seen it happen. In this chapter I will give you strategies you can use to handle any unexpected events without taking your head out of the game.

Work History and Education Issues

Before the interview, you should have prepared how to address any work experiences outside the norm. Even if you are not asked about the situation, the interview panel may wonder about what's written, or not written, on your resume. If you have employment gaps, they will wonder if you were fired. If you're switching companies, they will wonder why. If you're moving cities, they will wonder about the circumstances. They may not ask, but they will wonder.

I've interviewed people before who anticipated the interview team might have questions about something in their background. They made sure to mention the situation at some point in the interview. When done well, this is usually the best strategy, but it does depend on what occurred. When there is an understandable reason for an employment transition, explaining the situation prevents the team from speculating something terrible happened. Second, if you know it's going to come out during your reference check or background review, it will make you look like a liar if you haven't at least mentioned something about it.

Keep in mind one caveat, however. Mentioning the situation in the interview is not the same as covering it in great detail. Your goal is to address whatever happened and put a positive spin on it, to the extent you can. With that said, here are some suggestions about how to address common background issues:

Situation #1: You were fired. You need to find out if your former employer will give out any information about your employment there. If you know that their policy is only to give date of hire, position, and the date you left (which is the policy for many companies now), then you need not say, *I was fired.*

Instead, when explaining why you left the position, say something which is truthful yet not descriptive. If you are interviewing for management-level positions, you should say, *I enjoyed my work there. When I left, there were some disagreements regarding the focus of my efforts. I'm now looking for an opportunity where I can be more aligned with the strategic direction.*

If you are interviewing for line-level/support positions, you can be even more vague. Say, *I learned a lot in the job. Now I'm ready to take what I learned and have a new experience with a different employer.*

If you know your former employer is going to say you were fired if asked when part of a background check, you have to give more explanatory details. Do not bash you former employer, and do not say anything negative about why they fired you. Focus on a positive future and what you learned. You can say, *My former employer disagreed with some key decisions I made. Ultimately, they had to let me go. I understood completely. It's important for everyone on the team to be on the same page. That's why now I'm looking for an opportunity where I can be more aligned with the direction of the company.*

If they don't ask you explicitly why you left the company or why you're making a move, you should bring it up at the end. You can say, *You might be wondering why I left (X) company...* Then give your explanation. In the absence of information, people will make up stories in their heads that are probably far worse than what actually occurred. If you say nothing, it might be a red flag for the interview team. If you don't provide an explanation, it will remain a question mark.

Deliver your explanation with confidence. Don't go into details, and don't apologize or give the impression you did something bad. People get fired for all sorts of reasons. It's not uncommon, especially in private industry. Your goal is to provide the simplest explanation possible while remaining honest.

Situation #2: It's been a long time since you've worked, due to being laid off or fired. In this case, your goal is to ensure that people know you've been working hard doing *something* since you were last employed. You will still need to mention why you left. You definitely want to explain your departure if you were laid off, if your company dissolved, or if your company was acquired and a new management team cleaned house. These are all perfectly acceptable employment separation reasons.

When you explain your departure, the interview panel won't wonder if it was for a different, less ideal, reason. In the interview, after you've explained why you left, be sure to list the activities you have been pursuing while you've been unemployed.

When actively looking for work, hopefully you were networking, doing volunteer work, and maybe even consulting. Now is the time to talk about that work. What you want to avoid is having the interview team assume you've applied to hundreds of jobs and been rejected by many employers. An example might be, *When I left (X) company, I took some time to analyze the type of environment I wanted to work in. I have been very particular about where I have chosen to apply because I want to be certain it's the right match. While I've been considering my options, I've been volunteering at (X), doing some consulting/temporary work, and helping out at my child's school.*

Situation #3: You're re-entering the job market after being a stay at home parent. Your answer to this question is going to be dependent on the length and type of experience you had prior to staying home with the kids. If you had only entry-level experience when you left, you can usually leverage much of your parenting and managing the household experience to provide examples in the interview. Hopefully part of your experience included volunteer work where you managed projects or events and had to work well with others. That type of experience translates well into many entry-level positions.

If you had extensive professional-level experience prior to raising children, you will need to have some evidence in your answers that you have remained current in your line of work. It's helpful if you engaged in some contract work, consulting work or temporary work in order to show recent experience. Pursue those opportunities at least a year in advance of returning to full-time work.

In your answers, give examples from your prior work history and then add how or why it's still relevant today. The interview team will need you to make it explicit that you've continued learning while home. Do your best to show that with the time away, you can reflect more wisely upon your past experiences.

Situation #4: You don't have the education level preferred or even required. Sometimes you will get an interview without meeting the education qualifications. This usually happens because there aren't enough qualified candidates who have the education, and you have a high level of experience. It is my recommendation that you don't mention your lack of education at all unless asked. If you made it past the screening person, then there is no reason to highlight for the interview team that you're missing a preferred qualification.

If you did go to a college or university of some type, feel free to mention something you learned. If you are very close to earning your degree (within six months), then you *should* mention that in your intro comments. Otherwise, focus all your examples on specific work experiences. That will usually speak for itself if you've gotten to the interview stage.

If you are asked directly about your lack of a degree, your answer should focus on the positive while acknowledging the importance of higher education. After all, if they ask you to talk about it, they must believe it is important. You can say something like, *I think higher education is really important. If I could go back and do it again, I would certainly have gotten a degree. But when I was focused on beginning my career, it wasn't a barrier, and I was getting promoted without it. So, all of my learning came from direct experience. However, I've kept myself educated in other ways, such as* _____ . In this way, you explain that you value education, that you have experience in lieu of the degree, and that you have continued to educate yourself. Remain positive and project an unworried demeanor so that the interview team believes in your abilities without a degree.

Situation #5: You've had one or more jobs where you left after a short tenure. If you're someone who has switched companies several times over the last ten to fifteen years, you run the risk of being perceived as someone who can't get along with others. The interview panel may assume you're never satisfied and won't stay at their company. Worse, people may assume that you never last long at a job because you get fired.

If you only had one instance, you can probably leave it unaddressed. If the positions are all promotions, especially with the same company, you're equally safe. Everyone understands moving for a promotion. But if you've had short tenures in the same level of job, you definitely need to offer an explanation. A common and very understandable reason is that you were a trailing spouse and had to move with your husband or wife. If your moves were within one geographic area, however, that's not going to work.

Whether they ask you directly or not, you should have a good answer to explain the frequent job changes. Use it at the beginning or at the end of the interview, saying, *You may be wondering why it looks like I can't hold a job for more than two years,* in a joking tone.

The most important thing is the truth behind why you moved jobs so often. Use that. It could be that you were the person who came in to clean up a departmental mess, and then left because different leadership was needed after you accomplished your task. Maybe you really do enjoy challenges and found that unless you switched companies, you didn't have the same passion for your work. Follow that up by saying you are looking for a company that provides ongoing challenges so that you can stay energized.

As with all of my other advice, your own demeanor will make a difference to the interview panel. If you seem defensive and you blame others, you will not get the job. If you focus on your preferences and your own decision-making, you will have a much better chance.

Situation #6: You took a real or a perceived demotion. A real demotion is within the same company. For example, you went from being a vice president to being a director. A perceived demotion is if your title change looks like it was a demotion, when in reality it was a job with more pay. If the demotion was real and involuntary, use the same strategies as you would if you had been fired. Be positive, explain how much better it worked out for you, and share what you learned from the experience.

A demotion that was involuntary is much better than actually being fired. In fact, it tells your future employer that you obviously didn't do anything too bad, since your former employer wanted to keep you in some fashion. If the demotion was real, but voluntary, definitely say that it was your choice. Usually those occur because of family obligations. I recommend sharing the information up-front while adding that the family issues have now been resolved. Maybe you had a sick parent or child. Maybe your spouse's career needed to take precedence at that time period. Just make sure that if you're now applying to move up the ladder, that concern is no longer present.

If you moved companies, moving from a vice president to a director, you may not need to explain anything. If you subsequently rose through the ranks in the second company, the interview panel will interpret that it was a good move for you. If asked about it, or if it fits in your overall introductory answer, then be honest. Tell them, *I went from being a vice president to being a director, but my scope of responsibility was the same. There were just differences in how the positions were leveled at each company. The director position at Company X actually paid more than the vice president position at Company Y. Money isn't everything, but it was a great opportunity to get a new experience and at a higher salary range.*

If you're applying for a position that seems like a demotion to your potential employer, they may want to know the reason behind that as well. I once interviewed a principal who was seeking to be an assistant principal. She went out of her way to talk about her choice in her letter, and explained it in more detail to me over the phone. With a glowing reference check, it worked out for her, and she was hired.

I personally applied for a job that my future employer assumed paid much less than I was making, which made them wonder if they could afford my salary. I let them know through back channels what my then-current salary was. The future employer then realized it would be a promotion for me to be hired there.

Situation #7: You've been at one company for a long time and you've never received a promotion, remaining at the same level. If you don't explain what happened, the interview panel will think you're not a good candidate for promotion. They will assume that you applied for many promotions and didn't get any, and they will wonder why your previous company didn't promote you.

You must have a plausible reason for not promoting. I recommend that you provide a very brief statement about your roles when you give an overview of your experience at the beginning of the interview. Explain how each of your roles was slightly different. Even if you were in the same exact role for several years, highlight the depth of your knowledge as well as the many situations you learned about and successfully addressed.

Let the interview team know that there was value in your stability. Use it as a strength. If you were in the same position for a long time, you probably went through many bosses. Use that to show how adaptable you are. Do not mention anything about being bitter for not being promoted.

Let the panel assume it was your choice. Tell them that you've now decided you want different experiences in another company because you are engaged and get energized about fresh ideas and experiences.

For any less than ideal situations, put yourself in the mind of the potential employer. Anticipate what questions they might have. When talking about difficult situations in interviews, develop an honest but brief answer. Deliver it with authenticity and positivity in your voice.

Unexpected Events

I could have titled this section S**t Happens. That's really what it's about. Unexpected events do occur, even if you've prepared and planned the best you can. Mary Poppins can call herself practically perfect in every way, but even she had bad days, I'm sure. The random chaos of things that occur in our world is really annoying. It's especially irritating to those of us who do plan, plan, plan with the hope of avoiding mishaps and mayhem.

If you haven't figured it out yet (and if you're reading this at the age of 22 you might not have), you simply cannot control everything. Sometimes you trip and fall. Sometimes you'll spill your coffee in your lap. Sometimes your phone will ring when you thought it was on silent. Sometimes your alarm doesn't go off although you checked it three times. And sometimes, these things happen when you are interviewing for a new job. It sucks, I know.

If one of these unexpected events occurs during your interview, here is a little reassurance. How you react will tell the interview team way more about you than the random occurrence itself. Depending how you handle the situation, for most events listed, you will be able to recover and still do a great job in the interview. For occurrences that aren't really fixable, you may in fact not get the job because of what happened. If that's the case, the only thing you can do is laugh it off and move on.

You might be saying, *Whaaaaat? Laugh it off when I really wanted that job???* My answer is yes. Laugh it off. If you did all you could to prepare and a weird event occurred, then clearly-- very, very clearly—God has an entirely different plan for you. Laugh it off, shake it off, and move on. There are some ways to handle these events, however, which will help your chances of having a successful interview regardless.

Having a sense of humor, even if it's laughing at yourself, is a good strategy. Not judging yourself and avoiding negative self-talk is an *essential* strategy. As the song goes, shit really does happen. Here are some ideas about how to deal when it does.

1. Tripping and falling. If you're a man, you should be thinking, *This could be worse. I could be wearing a dress.* You might even say that. Do make some sort of funny comment if you trip and fall. It depends on the situation, but use something like, *Wow those floors are sure shiny and slippery! You must spend a fortune on your cleaning company!* Sometimes, *Sorry, first day with my new feet* can work as well. Make it funny and self-deprecating.

2. Someone spills water or coffee during the interview. First, try to keep your beverages away from your hands while you're interviewing. But if it happens to you, or to someone on the interview team, don't let it bother you. People will jump up to find towels, and you'll be interrupted. Just stay centered and you will be fine. If someone else spilled, be sure to say, *Oh, no problem, it gives me some more time to think about that last question*, while smiling. If you spilled, you can say, *So sorry, I guess I got really excited about that last question!* If offered towels, help clean up.

3. You spill coffee or water on yourself at a time when you have no choice but to enter the interview room with it on you. All you can do is make a joke like, *Normally I'm drinking coffee. I don't usually wear it into the interview.* Definitely say something that explains the stain on your shirt or suit. It's fine to say, *Well this is really embarrassing, but this stain on my shirt is the coffee (water) I spilled on myself while waiting. At work, I normally keep a clean shirt in my office just for this type of emergency.*

If you spill on your shirt in your car, hopefully you followed my advice for leaving early. Then you can probably stop at a Walgreens, a department store, or other location to get a new one. This may be easier for women who can wear nearly anything under a suit and hide it. For men, finding a collared shirt and tie might be difficult unless your interview is near a department store. All the more reason to keep a spare one in the car during your job search.

4. Chairs or interview couches uncomfortable for your shape or size. There are all kinds of body shapes and sizes. Sometimes the environments we interview in simply aren't conducive to a physically comfortable interview. I try to make sure that interview chairs are comfortable for all sizes, but even I can encounter space limitations.

People on the shorter side may find chairs that aren't quite tall enough. People on the tall side may find that their legs barely fit under the table. And people on the larger size may find chairs with arms that don't really accommodate a wider berth. Then there are the couches you encounter occasionally when you're meeting one-on-one in people's offices. Those can be impossible to get out of unless you've been doing squat repetitions at exercise class. The point is, if you're not a completely average size, you can count on some aspect of the interview being uncomfortable.

To counteract that, have a few advance strategies in mind. If you're a larger person, plan to sit on the edge of the chair if your body size won't fit between the armrests. Practice doing this at home with a chair that rolls. It's not going to be comfortable, but practicing helps. If you walk into the interview room and see an unused chair that would be more comfortable for you, feel free to say, while smiling, *Hey do you mind if I switched chairs? That one looks a little more comfortable for me.* Deliver this request smiling without one hint of shame or guilt, and you'll be fine.

I find that larger people sometimes project a lack of confidence due to their size. Perhaps they believe people are judging them harshly. If you are large, generate enough confidence to own the room. Don't shrink into the room, making yourself seem small. Whether you're happy with your current weight or trying to lose weight, be confident in your skills. Asking for another chair is not going to hinder your job chances, and (unless the interview is for a health and fitness manager job!), the interview team will likely be impressed by your confidence.

If you are much taller than average, you probably cannot do much about the table height. If it's the type of chair that swivels, try swiveling it slightly to one side so that your legs have room to the side of the table. If the panel is far enough away from you at the table, you can just put your legs out straight under the table without risk of playing footsie with other panel members. If that does happen, laugh it off saying, *Sorry! With my height that happens all the time!*

I am not taller than average, but one time the interview team was so close to me that I did think I had kicked one of the panel members. I just stopped and said, "Oh my gosh I feel like I just kicked someone under the table, did I?" As it turns out, the answer was no--there was a middle barrier under the table. However, if I had not stopped to say something, it would have been rolling around in my head during the interview. I checked because I didn't want it distracting me.

If you are very short, you have a different problem. Hopefully, the chair they put you in will adjust up or down. Don't be shy about moving the chair up if it will. However, if you move it up too far, your feet may not hit the ground. On the other hand, if it doesn't move, you might feel like you're looking up over the table. Neither are going to help your confidence. Thus, you need to bring a back-up strategy with you!

If you're a man, buy the thickest briefcase you can find, and walk in with it. If you're a woman, do the same thing with a purse or satchel. For either, put a few books in it to keep it sturdy. Smile, saying, *Oh this happens to me all the time. I'm always having to adjust to fit my height* or *They only make these chairs for average people!*

If your feet don't touch the ground, move your briefcase or purse under your feet once you've adjusted the chair. Then your feet will have something to rest on. You can probably do this without them even knowing. If you can't move the chair, you'll say something similar, such as, *My briefcase (purse) always helps out in these situations, no problem!* Then put your briefcase or purse on the chair and plop yourself right down on it. As soon as the interview team sees that you have no problem with your height, they won't either.

The last piece of advice I have on this topic is about generally uncomfortable couches. For some reason I have yet to fathom, the ones you see in an executive's office are impossibly low. They certainly don't make for graceful departures, no matter what your body type is (although, for shorter people, this may be a welcome break for you). When you are getting up, use the strategy of turning your body slightly and using one hand to push yourself up. If you really have been doing your squats in exercise class, you can probably stand right up.

For those of us who think a nice walk around the block is exercise, don't try to get up all at once. Otherwise, you run the risk of literally falling back into the couch. If that does happen, you might joke, *Is this part of the interview? Was it a test to see if I could get out of this couch? If so I obviously failed!* Be sure to laugh when you say it so that the interviewer knows how much confidence you have.

In short, body shape inconveniences are best handled with humor and confidence. Use your visualizations and confidence builders before the interview. Also do some meditating or thinking about the body shape issues you do have. Put any negative thoughts in that box of insecurities you're going to push into the ocean or burn in your backyard. How you feel about yourself will be evident in the interview, so love yourself and your body!

5. Your phone goes off during the interview. Obviously, you would have turned off your phone before the interview. But then the phone gremlins decide, nah, you didn't turn it off. So it rings. Make a joke about who is calling. If you're interviewing at Microsoft, you could say, *Oh sorry that must be Bill Gates returning my call.* You could also say, *FINALLY, Matt Lauer (or your favorite celebrity) is calling me back!* Then you will apologize and reassure them that you thought the phone was off.

Once I was leading a panel interview. A young man seeking a promotion had the kind of company phone that also operates like a walkie-talkie. It went off once, and he said, "Oh I'm so sorry, I thought for sure I turned it off!" He did something to the phone. Then the phone went off AGAIN. The young man took out the phone, looked at it with disgust, walked to the door and dropped the phone outside the door. He joked, "If it wasn't a company phone I would have thrown the darn thing. OK, now there shouldn't be any more interruptions! I'm so sorry!" The team laughed as he sat back down, ready to finish the interview.

6. Missed the interview time. Oh, the best laid plans. You know you wrote down the right interview time and day. You added it to your calendar. But then it turns out something went wrong. Either you wrote it down wrong, or the employer switched it and forgot to tell you. Maybe you actually get into a car accident on your way to the interview and there is no way you can make it on time.

In this case, all you can do is call, explain the situation and beg for an alternative time. Sometimes it just won't work at the company end. However, if you were one of their top candidates, they will make it work. If they don't give you an option to reschedule, console yourself with the fact that you may only have had an outside chance anyway.

7. The interview panel is comprised of someone with whom you've had a contentious relationship. Maybe the person truly hates you. Maybe it was just one or two bad experiences. You will need to act as if nothing is amiss. If whatever happened was relatively minor but something for which you shared fault, you could try to subtly weave in your regret. Use it in an example that requires reflection about something you would have done differently. Don't mention the incident directly, and don't treat that person in an odd manner. Keep the same level of eye contact with that person. Smile and greet the person as if nothing occurred.

Unless it is a one-on-one interview, the person is one voice in the panel, and may possibly be overruled. You can hope that the person is reasoned enough to give you another chance. However, if that person has a negative opinion of you, it will be difficult to get to the next level. Let it go and move on.

Making a big deal about it to human resources will only call attention to that person's dislike of you. If the employer is a big company and you ignore it, you will hopefully still have an opportunity to interview for other jobs. At some point, maybe that person will have left the company. What you don't want to do is throw a fit about the interview being unfair. This will leave a bad impression also on the human resources team. It can also call attention to an incident that may not be widely known.

8. Getting interrupted by a fire alarm, fire drill, food being brought in to the interview team, or other random disruption. These events have the potential to inhibit your train of thought and throw you off your game. Don't let that happen. Keep smiling, make a joke, and wait for the questions to restart. I once had to walk a candidate out of the building for a fire drill. The person was so relaxed that it ended up being a good time for her to make an even better impression on me. For most jobs, you'll be expected to handle minor interruptions daily. Demonstrating that these little problems don't bother you, and that you can maintain your confidence and poise, will add to the interview team's positive opinion of you.

9. You understand the question, but you have absolutely no clue what the answer might be. Questions like this are usually related to very specific technical content about which you have no knowledge. An example would be, *Tell us your opinion about the impact of Sarbanes-Oxley on the technology sector's ability to sustain increasing revenue.* If you know very little about what Sarbanes-Oxley is, you're stuck with a question you cannot answer.

First, buy yourself some time. Think for a moment, and then ask them to repeat the question. While they are repeating the question, try to identify anything in the question you can comment upon. For example, if you know the technology sector and at least know that Sarbanes-Oxley is a law related to finances, you could say, *Although I am aware of several laws that have the potential to impact the technology sector, such as _____, I'm not totally familiar with the provisions of*

Sarbanes-Oxley. Would you mind giving me a brief overview so that I can provide you a full answer with my analysis?

If you don't know whether Sarbanes-Oxley is a law or a new video game, you're going to have to change your approach: *Although of course I'm familiar with a number of issues impacting the technology industry, I'm not totally familiar with Sarbanes-Oxley. Would you mind giving me the context of it so that I can answer fully?* Unfortunately, if the interviewer says, *I'm sorry, we can't give you that information*, then you'll have to answer the question as best you can. In this example, that would mean focusing on impacts other than Sarbanes-Oxley. It's true that you won't have answered the question, but at least you will be able to show them you are able to analyze other impacts.

10. *You start to answer a question and in the middle of it your brain completely goes blank.* This happens a lot in interviews, even to people who have an otherwise stellar performance. The worst thing you can do is let it take you off your rhythm. Avoid letting it force you down a path that isn't even related to the answer you began to provide. Instead, if you draw a blank, stop yourself. Smile at the interview team and say, *I'm so sorry. I didn't think I was nervous but maybe I am! My mind just went completely blank. Could you please repeat the question?* Another alternative is to stop and smile, then say, *I think I may have gotten off topic. Could you please repeat the question so I can be sure to fully answer it?*

Take the Shortcut

1. Questions about a less than ideal work history should be answered honestly but not with a lot of detail.

2. Never be negative about a former employer, boss, or work situation.

3. Handle unexpected accidents or events with humor. Keep your focus by joking about them and realizing they are usually minor events that will have no impact on the interview team's opinion about you.

4. How you handle unexpected events will give the interview team important information about how you might handle a real work situation that doesn't go well. Demonstrate confidence at all times.

Chapter Six

Tips for Different Interview Formats

In my book *Ready for Take-Off,* I provide specific advice regarding alternative interview formats and how you should prepare content for them. This chapter will take each of the formats and tell you more about what to wear, what to do, and what not to do in each setting. The four main formats are behavioral event interviewing, group interviews, "coffee chat" interviews, and phone interviews.

Behavioral Event Interviews

The hiring manager will ask you a very broad question. Then he may probe your answer by following up on more specific questions. These questions could be judging several of your traits or skills. The theory behind behavioral event interviews is that they tend to level the playing field between those who are natural talkers and those who might be a little more reserved.

Behavioral event questions focus on specific examples or events that have actually occurred. Interviewers using this strategy do not care about what you might do. They want to know about actual events that occurred. Thus, use the following strategies.

1. Be sure to distinguish behaviors that you personally did or led. Avoid the use of "we" unless it truly was a group effort.

2. Always describe the situation in detail while also explaining the reasoning behind why you chose specific strategies.

3. Be sure to explain what you did, what you were considering or thinking about when you did it, why you eventually decided on a specific course of action, and what the end result was.

4. Include pertinent details regarding how you handled difficult circumstances such as delays, roadblocks or personality differences.

5. End the question by explaining what you learned from the experience or how you applied it in other settings.

Group Interviews

Group interviews are when many candidates are in the same room together, answering questions in front of each other. They are quite common when companies need to hire multiple candidates at a time. Companies also use this technique when they want to see how candidates interact with each other in a large group. In these instances, sometimes the company will give you a project or problem you need to work on together. Then they will observe how you interact with others. Group interviews are becoming more and more common. If you know you're going to be in a group interview situation, prepare by reviewing these strategies to help you be successful.

1. Be poised but not cold, friendly but not creepy. Smile and greet everyone and act excited to meet new people. This will also help your mind get ready for the process. The company may be watching you interact with others before you even arrive.

2. Make eye contact with every person in the room. Treat everyone as if they are interviewers. During the interview, one interviewer may not say anything, taking notes with no expression. Include that person in your eye contact.

3. During the interview, demonstrate you are engaged and confident by sitting up straight, nodding, and smiling.

4. If you took time in the beginning to learn the names of your fellow candidates, show personalized attention to them during the process. Say things like, *I loved what James just said, and I'd like to expand on that answer by saying...*

5. Be polite. Use your manners. Don't speak over people. If you do accidentally interrupt, apologize. If you notice that one person in the group hasn't said anything, you might say, *I'd love to answer this question, but I feel like Ryan hasn't had a chance to speak yet, so I think I'll pass this to him.* Every organization wants a good team player. Being polite and making sure to include everyone will impress the interviewers.

6. Be articulate. Use your memorized examples and answers just as if you were the only interviewee. However, you may need to shorten some of them to accommodate other group members. Thus, give the meat of your prepared answers but in a more succinct way, leaving out less important details.

7. For women, wear pants if you know you're going to be in a group interview. You may not have the benefit of a table. Instead, you likely will be sitting in a circle of chairs. Ensure you don't have to worry about flashing anyone by wearing pants instead of a skirt.

The Coffee Chat Interview

Often companies will schedule less formal interactions with potential coworkers. These interactions are designed to determine if you will fit in as part of a team. They may occur over coffee, while touring the facility/location, or even in the car on the way to pick you up. Sometimes you're invited to have lunch or dinner. In addition to maintaining a friendly, yet professional demeanor, adhere to these guidelines.

1. Make sure your answers in the informal setting are consistent throughout all of the interview formats. Candidates can make mistakes by providing more details or alternate examples that are not helpful to the selection process.

2. Stay positive. Do not get so comfortable that you demonstrate negative personality traits when in an informal setting. Avoid being sarcastic, talking poorly about a former employer, or complaining about an annoying coworker.

3. Use good manners. You will be judged if you use bad manners while eating. Don't talk with your mouth full, be sure to use a napkin, and say please and thank you to the restaurant/coffee servers.

4. Don't order messy food. Remember, you're being interviewed. Don't order finger food that will require you to constantly wipe off your hands or lick your fingers. Even some salads have vegetables so loud that they aren't a wise choice. Order anything that is soft, not messy, and that you can eat with a fork. Lasagna, chicken enchiladas, salmon, and burgers without buns are all good options.

5. Hold up your end of the conversation. Prepare in advance to ask the person about the company and their role. Be sure to think about the flow of the conversation and how

you will contribute to the back and forth. People love to talk about themselves. Ask questions like, *How long have you worked here?* and *What's your favorite thing about working here?* These questions work well to elicit a positive response.

6. Smile genuinely. Your smile will leave a strong impression that you are a positive team player. Smiling also helps you be more relaxed.

7. Dress appropriately. Even though "coffee chat" interviews are designed as less formal, it's still an interview. Although you may be able to avoid wearing a full business suit, you still need to wear either a dress/jacket or shirt/tie combination. Depending on where you're going, you might also choose less formal shoes. Make sure they are new, polished, and not dirty.

Skype or FaceTime Interviews

To avoid travel costs before a finalist round, Skype and FaceTime can be used to narrow down large pools of candidates in order to determine who will move on to an in-person interview. Depending on the level of position, this technology might also be used for final selection. Either way, use these strategies to make the best impression you can.

1. Use an appropriate backdrop. The best option is a bare wall. If you don't have that option, be sure whatever is behind you isn't going to distract the team. Using FaceTime, I once interviewed a candidate who was sitting. Behind him were framed posters with famous quotes on them. That normally would be fine. However, in this case, the quotes were odd, and some on the interview team

found them strange. Others judged them as slightly offensive.

2. Work extra hard to connect to the team. If you can't see the whole team together, be sure to use names in order to connect. You can make jokes, like, *Staci, I don't see you but I'm sure you're nodding about me including human resources in the decision!* Sometimes you'll need to move your head slightly toward the person asking the question, so they know you're making eye contact. Be sure not to spend all your time looking up or down while answering, which is easy to do when people aren't in the room with you.

3. Avoid using extra references or looking at notes. Just because you're not in the same room doesn't mean the panel can't see you. Looking at pages of notes or other materials you wouldn't normally bring to an in-person interview is not recommended.

4. Dress appropriately. You should dress the same as you would for a normal interview. If you have bad luck and get called for an interview while on a beach vacation, ask your hotel concierge to help you locate a shirt and tie to wear. You can purchase something or, if you're lucky, borrow it from the staff at the hotel. The interview team will judge you negatively if what they see isn't business attire.

Take the Shortcut

1. Be aware that different interview formats require slightly different strategies.

2. Make sure your attire is appropriate yet comfortable relative to the interview format.
3. No matter what the interview format, smiling, connecting to the interviewer, and being prepared with thoughtful responses and questions of your own will help you be successful.

Chapter Seven

---

40 Don'ts

I have interviewed hundreds of candidates over my twenty years in human resources. Based on that experience, I've created a list of mistakes people make in interviews. These mistakes distract the team from hearing the candidate's words. Don't think of the list as prohibitions. Think of them as cautions. If you make one mistake, your interview is not going to be over. Interview panels understand that people are nervous and may have quirks that they don't normally show.

Many people who I eventually hired made one or more of these mistakes. However, their overall preparation, experience, and answers far outweighed any mistakes they might have made on the following list. When you are interviewing, your goal is to focus on doing things right. If you can avoid making any of these silly mistakes, it just adds to your chances of getting the job. I've provided explanations for these behaviors you should try to avoid. Many didn't seem to require more than a brief explanation. If you want more clarification on any item I didn't explain well, just email me at stacimcintosh23@gmail.com.

The 40

1. Assuming the whole team knows you as well as some of the team. Sometimes we interview with people we have worked with in the past. Even if you are interviewing with five people who you know very well, pretend as if you don't know them and give full, detailed answers. I've seen many internal candidates lose jobs because they assumed that the interview panel knew their thinking and experiences. Then an external candidate interviewed and blew them out of the water. Don't let that be you.

2. Giving the impression you think you have the job. In many interview situations, some candidates believe with certainty that they will be selected. Usually they have good reason to believe so. Their boss has told them. Their coworkers have told them. They know they are the heir apparent. Do not, ever, give the impression or assume that you have the job. Everyone in your work unit may love you, but the larger company may believe it's time for a change. You never know. Plus, if an external candidate comes in and hits it out of the park, and *your* interview is just ho-hum, you could miss out on the job. Always bring your best game.

3. Being arrogant, not humble. No one wants a know-it-all for a co-worker.

4. Being disorganized in your answers. See my book *Ready for Take-Off* if you need more detailed help in how to organize your answers.

5. Using vague phrases that say very little. Using phrases such as *Communication is key* and *We just kept working at it* and *Using collaboration in that situation is best* don't tell the interview team much about the specific strategies you would use. Rather than making broad sweeping statements, list specific actions. Rather than say, *Communication is key* you would instead say, *I ensure there is constant communication by personally contacting each person for feedback, sending detailed summaries of meetings, and following up personally if anyone expresses a concern.*

6. Appearing "frenetic", "frantic" or "hyper". Show enthusiasm without seeming out of control.

7. Giving all philosophy and no specifics. Interviewers will wonder if you're all talk and no action.

8. Giving all specifics and no philosophy. Interviewers will wonder if you're so much of a do-er that you never think about strategy.

9. Name dropping the wrong name. Or even the right name. Once while I was leading an interview panel, we asked the candidate who had been the person who had influenced him the most in his career. Rather than choosing a relatively famous person, a national leader, or even an obscure author, the candidate mentioned a local woman well known in that industry. The person was well respected by most of her peers. However, one very influential person on the panel, the one with the most hiring authority, had been involved in a very negative experience with the woman the candidate mentioned. Needless to say, the candidate did not get the job. Avoid using or mentioning any names that aren't completely neutral when using examples in your interview.

10. Asking too many questions at the end of the interview. Pay attention to the time allotted for the interview. When called to schedule the interview, ask how much time you should plan for. If, at the end of the interview, you know you've gone over, ask one question at most. Normally, two questions are about right. Be prepared for three or four just in case they keep prompting you. If you don't know, ask two questions and then make your fabulous closing statement.

11. Not using the end of the interview to make a great closing statement. Just like the end of a great novel, your last statement should leave the interview team feeling knowledgeable about you while at the same time connected to you.

12. Appearing nervous instead of confidant. Re-read Chapter One if necessary.

13. Not striking a balance between relationships and accountability. Make sure your answers overall contain a little of both. If you're always talking about ways to hold people accountable for results, you'll seem mean. Along with holding people accountable, also talk about collaboration, helping employees, and getting along.

14. Appearing to have no independent thought. After a day of interviewing similar people using the same questions, interview teams get weary of common answers and similar examples. Make sure you bring some interesting thoughts to the interview. Weave in current reading, research, or even lesser known facts into your answers.

15. Insulting the geographic location or the organization's decisions in some way. This is not the time to give your unfiltered opinion of the city or a recent company decision you felt was wrong. Stay positive.

16. "Kitchen sinking" your answers. This is when you hear a topic and you throw every random fact you know about it into your answer, regardless of relevance. Be thoughtful about having a main point and supporting examples.

17. Not paying attention to the time and how long you're answering each question. Plan to spend about three to four minutes answering each question. Any more, and you're going to run out of time. Any less, and you're probably not providing a full enough answer. In a 45-minute interview, you can guess there will be an opening question, seven to eight content questions, and one prompt to ask if you have questions. Wear a big watch you can glance at discreetly to know if you're taking too long. You won't always be in a room where you can see a clock. The interview team will tune you out if they think you're rambling. Another tip: if you're with a panel and they all quit writing notes, it's time to end your answer.

18. Appearing bored, tired, and/or lacking energy. That is how the team will judge your future performance as a coworker.

19. Asking pay, benefit, vacation, and working conditions questions in the interview. Save it for when you get the job offer. It takes away the time from selling yourself to the team. In private companies, let them fall in love with you first, and then they will try hard to get the salary you need. For public sector positions, the pay ranges are usually less flexible. However, salary scales are also readily available, so do ask first to see if the pay is within your range before interviewing.

20. Being too mechanical in your interview technique. Yes, you should be organized, but if all of your answers sound oddly the same and don't sound natural, you won't connect.

21. Appearing disheveled or wrinkled, dressing oddly, wearing an odd color, or showing odd personal appearance choices. As I shared in the Interview Etiquette chapter, iron your clothes, wear conservative attire, don't be flashy, and don't make quirky accessory, clothing or personal appearance choices. Stay away from anything glittery or sparkly that is going to distract from what you're saying.

22. Using brands, mascots, or special wording to match with the place you're interviewing. Making subtle connections can be helpful. Constantly using or referring to the company brand, logos, or vision statement will make you seem overeager and possibly weird.

23. Complimenting the team on each question asked. One or two *That's a great question* comments are fine. Every question, and it's very distracting.

24. Wearing too much perfume, aftershave, or cologne. It's best if you don't smell, even if you think you smell good.

25. Not telling the truth, the whole truth, and nothing but the truth. Making up events or experiences will most likely come back to haunt you. If you get through the reference check, your untruths will still eventually become apparent.

26. Taking credit for things you didn't do. I've had people do this even when interviewing at the company they worked at. Again, it can end up making you seem like a liar or an egomaniac.

27. Not taking credit for accomplishments you led. Collaborative and inclusive cultures are great. But if you led a specific initiative, action, or strategy, use the word "I" and not "we". Otherwise, the interview team will view you only as a participant and not a leader. Obviously, this applies more to management/leader positions than line-level positions.

28. Blaming others for problems you encountered. This is a job opportunity killer. Being negative is bad enough. Blaming others for your problems flags to the interview team that you *did* have problems in your previous position. Worse yet, you are taking no responsibility for them.

29. Demonstrating an obvious lack of knowledge about the place you're interviewing for, or the job. True confession here. I had a recruiter call me and leave a message. I called back thinking he was scheduling an interview. He wasn't. He proceeded to ask me questions regarding what I knew about the company. I couldn't web-search fast enough while I was talking, and, needless to say, that possibility was over.

30. Writing down the entire question before answering. Writing down any portion of the question can put off some interview teams. For that reason, I advise against it unless you really need it. Jotting down a few phrases to help you remember the question is usually acceptable. Having the questioner slow down so you can write out every word is going to prevent you from getting the job.

31. Having your cell phone go off during the interview. Hey, it happens. But if it does, you had better joke about it and make it clear that you swore you had turned it off.

32. Reading a text from your teenager or your ride. Put your phone away. Period. No vibrating, or put it on airplane mode. If necessary, warn your friends and family that they will not be able to reach you during that time period. If you really need to, give the landline or email of the actual office that scheduled you, in case of emergency. Just be aware you run the risk of the panel viewing you as a worker who can't go 45 minutes without texting family. Not good.

33. Laughing more loudly or more obnoxiously than any member of the interview team. Go ahead and laugh, but if you're the loudest person in the room, tone it down. Also, if you make a statement you think was a joke, and no one else laughs, keep it to yourself. They didn't get it.

34. Referring to the numerous other interviews you've had and not gotten the job. There is no reason to bring up this fact. It makes you look like an undesirable candidate. The interview team will second-guess their decision if they do initially think they want to select you.

35. Saying the reason why you want the job is "I really just want to move from Pottersville." Being in a warm climate, we see this a lot in Las Vegas. It makes interview teams wonder if the person really wants to work for the company or if they simply want to move away from wherever they are at. Interview teams want to work with people who want to contribute to the organization, not just enjoy the climate.

36. Saying the reason why you want the job is "I can retire from my current job and come here." In concept, it's great if you can retire from one organization and go to work at another. Those of us who have government pensions get it. However, mentioning it in an interview makes panels assume you are not going to work hard. They will think you see this opportunity as, in essence, a retirement job. Focus on seeking a new challenge instead. If the job you want is clearly easier or a step down from your previous job, you can mention your retirement obliquely only. Say, *Since I'm able to retire from the Nevada system as an accountant, I'm really excited to be able to pursue another challenging career path.*

37. Going on and on when closing the interview. Your closing statement should be planned, rehearsed, eloquent, and to the point. Wandering on about various topics that may or may not have been asked in the interview makes the team long for an ending. This is not the impression you want to leave.

38. Chewing gum. Why, oh, why do I still have to mention this? Because people still do it.

39. Knowing too much information about the interview panel. If you manage to find commonalities, fine. If you know the name of each panel member's dog, you will seem like a cyber stalker.

40. Focusing on why the job will help you rather than how you will help the organization. Organizations want someone who will contribute. Never say you want a job because *It's the next logical step in my career.* Instead, focus on the opportunity to learn new insights while using your experience to contribute to the success of the company.

Take the Shortcut

1. You can avoid common interview mistakes by knowing what they are and avoiding committing them yourself.

2. One interview mistake is not going to prevent you from getting the job if you are great in every other way. But several mistakes in one interview will inhibit your job search.

3. In general, you want to avoid doing anything that might distract from your well rehearsed, thoughtful, and articulate answers.

Chapter Eight

Receiving Interview Feedback

Receiving feedback on your interview isn't fun. It's like giving someone a knife and asking them to open your vein. It's akin to saying, *You completely shook my confidence, ruined my week, and made a huge mistake not hiring me. Oh and also, could you please go into detail about how I f&*%-ed up?* For that reason, it's fairly rare for people to ask for feedback.

Nevertheless, it's the best way to know if you need to course correct your interview skills. If you do, you will be able to improve your interview skills immediately before future interviews. If you think you've mastered answering questions and exuding the correct amount of confidence, it's the only way to find out if you're right.

The good thing about feedback is that it can also verify what you feel about how you're doing. I've told people before that their interview skills were great. They only lacked the level of experience of the hired candidate. It makes you feel good to know that you made a good impression like you thought you did.

In addition to helping you improve your interview skills if you need to, feedback also is an excellent networking opportunity. If the person delivering the feedback states you did an excellent job, you can say, *Thank you so much for taking the time to talk with me. If you see any other positions in your company or in your network that you think I might be good for, I would really appreciate a referral.* Because you took the time to get feedback, the person will remember you more.

If you see a job posted you want to apply for in the same company, you can also reach out later. Ask the person who gave you feedback to put in a good word for you. A nice email would say, *Thank you for providing me feedback regarding my recent interview for _____. I saw a position posted at your company for (job title). I think my work experience matches the qualifications needed for that position. If you also think I might be a good candidate, I would very much appreciate you giving the hiring manager my name. Again, thank you so much for your help! Also, if you have any additional information or advice, I would love to hear from you again. Sincerely, John Doe.*

I receive many questions about how and from whom to ask for interview feedback. The best person to ask for feedback is the lead interviewer, even if that person isn't the highest-ranking in the room. Typically it's the person who called to schedule the interview (or the person whose assistant scheduled the interview). Many times it's a human resources manager or executive who sat in on the interviews. Always ask for feedback from someone who was in the interview. Generalized feedback human resources provides based on someone else's notes rarely gives robust insight.

It's best to get feedback as soon as possible, so do so when you are notified you didn't get the job. If you receive a call or email, respond right away. Say, *Of course I'm disappointed, but I would love to get some feedback so I can do better in other interviews. Would you be willing to give me your perspective regarding my interview skills? I would be happy to chat over the phone or schedule an appointment, whatever is easiest for you.*

If the person delivering the message wasn't on the interview team, you would change it to say, *Would Dr. McIntosh or another member of the interview team be willing to give their perspective regarding my interview skills?* No one minds it when candidates ask for feedback. Don't feel like you're imposing just by asking. They may tell you no, but at least you asked.

If you're lucky enough to have someone actually offer you feedback before you have to ask, always say yes. I usually only go out of my way to offer feedback when it's a candidate who I think has the potential to be a great employee in the future. I also offer when I think the candidate could be very competitive with some interview improvements.

I once interviewed a candidate "Josh" who had an energetic, but awful, interview. After the interview, when I told Josh he didn't get the job, he asked for some feedback. I always warn people in advance that when I give feedback, I can be brutally honest, and they might not like some of my opinions. With Josh, I knew it would sting more than usual. I forewarned him in more detail. He said he wanted me to be brutally honest. He emphasized that he could take it. Kindly but honestly, I gave him his feedback.

His energy was too over the top. He seemed weird. His presentation was gimmicky and wasn't professional enough. He was overly enthusiastic when greeting each individual and came across as invading their space. His answers were all over the place. He had a lot of great details and examples but they weren't organized in a comprehensible way. Based on his interview, I told him I didn't think he would be a match for our company in the near future.

To his credit, he listened intently, said he understood, and thanked me profusely for the feedback. He said he had done eight other interviews and hadn't gotten any of those jobs. "Now I know why," he said, sounding relieved, "No one has given me the level of detailed feedback you did. It actually feels better because I know I can improve this."

Less than a month later, Josh wrote to me. He told me that he had received the very next job he had interviewed for. He said he had written down everything I said and had practiced toning down his delivery and organizing his answers. He thanked me again, ending with, "I'm pretty sure I wouldn't have gotten this job either if it weren't for your advice." A year later when I saw him at a professional conference, he went out of his way to hug me. All of that would not have occurred if he had not asked for feedback.

Josh was unique in that he knew how to take feedback. Even when people learn to ask for feedback, they still don't know how to take it. For that reason, I have prepared a list of what to do, and what not to do, when asking for feedback.

Do's and Don't For Getting Feedback

1. Do take no for an answer. If the company declines to provide you with feedback, thank them for their time and move on. There is no benefit for you to push the issue.

2. Do ask for feedback, but only if you really want it and are in the mindset to hear opinions that you might not like. If you are not really going to work to use the feedback, it doesn't make sense to waste your time nor the company's time.

3. Do be prepared with some general questions to get the person started. I always start my feedback sessions asking what the person would like to know more about. Depending on how much they say, I will tailor the level of detail I provide to what I perceive is their mindset. A good question for candidates to ask is, *I would really like your perspective regarding how I could improve my interview skills overall and what I could have done better when I interviewed with your panel.* If the candidate starts with, *I thought I did great.*

I just want to know why I wasn't hired, I take that as an indication that he is not ready to hear that he was not great. You will not get candid feedback unless you seem open to hearing it.

4. Do be prepared with more specific questions for those who may be too nice to tell you anything negative. Not all people are able to give direct feedback that might hurt your feelings. If you sense that's the type of person you're talking to, you need to get more specific. Ask detailed questions such as, *Could you tell me if my answers were organized? Did I seem confident? Did my answers contain enough detail? Did I come across as nervous?* Even the nicest people will give you answers to detailed questions if you ask them.

5. Do nod, smile, and take notes to show you are listening, that you value the person's time, and that you appreciate the feedback. Ask clarifying questions if needed to show you are paying attention.

6. Do thank the person for their time. Follow up with a thank you note or email.

7. Do realize that just because you received feedback doesn't mean it's totally accurate. Feedback is only one person or one panel's perspective. What may be funny to one interview team may be annoying to another. This is why it's important to have perspective. Ask for feedback every time, and you can find common threads.

8. Do share the feedback you received with someone you trust to get another perspective. If the feedback rattled you, it's important for you not to let it shake your confidence in the next interview. Ask your trusted friend if the feedback might be accurate in some ways.

9. Do use the feedback to refine your performance, your answers, or your tone. But also, continue to be yourself. Just be the most articulate, confident, and polished version of yourself.

10. Do consider the feedback meeting part of a future selection process. You are leaving an impression that could help or hurt you for a future job. Every meeting you have with the company is part of the interview process.

11. Don't be defensive or try to explain yourself, even if you don't agree with the feedback. Once I gave a candidate feedback regarding how to organize answers to the questions. She told me that the reason her answers weren't organized was that the questions were too complicated. Defending yourself after you haven't gotten the job only makes you look argumentative and bitter.

12. Don't ever use the feedback meeting to complain about the hiring process being too long, too layered, or too confusing. All of that might be true, but if you complain about it, you will be leaving a poor impression on the company. I've had candidates email me as the human resources lead with suggestions for how the hiring manager should have done, or not done, this or that. Even if you're technically correct, you can bet that hiring manager is not going to consider you again for any other position. The time to help improve the process is after you've gotten the job, not while you're trying to get your foot in the door.

13. Don't use the feedback process to explain again how you really are the most qualified candidate. Don't ask, *What qualifications did the hired candidate have that I didn't?* Everyone who received an interview was qualified. By the time you get to that point, it's about finding the match for the company and the position. You will only make enemies if you challenge the company on its decision. Focus on

what you could do better, not on the selected candidate's relative qualifications.

14. Don't have your husband, wife, family members, church clergy, friends or neighbors ask for feedback about you. Also, never let them write letters advocating for why you should have gotten the job. This will make you look weak and unable to ask for your own feedback. It will also make the company suspect you could be a problem employee whose family members complain about everything. Your name will certainly stand out to company personnel in the future. But in a bad way, not a good way.

15. Don't sue the company nor file a discrimination claim unless three conditions are met. The first condition is that you have consulted an attorney who believes you have a discrimination claim. Even so, consider a claim only if the attorney is willing to take your case on contingency, meaning, he only gets paid if you get paid. The second condition is if you have reason to believe others have experienced discrimination or unequal treatment similar to yours. The final condition is if you're moving out of town or you already have another job.

Like you, I've read cases in the news where companies were found to have engaged in discriminatory hiring practices, either deliberate or inadvertent. It would be naive to think it never happens. However, it's very difficult to prove, and a lawsuit usually doesn't result in you getting hired. Rather, if you win, it results in you getting a payout, usually many years after the event. At the end of the conflict, you have to calculate if the money you received can be your income permanently. If your name is associated with a hiring lawsuit, other companies can find legal ways to avoid hiring you, even if you are proven to be right. If you believe you have been discriminated against for any reason, do your homework first before you invest time, energy, money, and possibly your reputation in a legal battle. I applaud those people who have the courage to stand up for their legal rights and for what they believe in. I just want to be sure they know what could be the result if they lose.

Take the Shortcut

1. Always ask for feedback after an interview and always accept feedback if it is offered.

2. No one is going to think poorly of you if you ask for feedback, even companies who don't provide it.

3. Only ask for feedback if you are ready to hear it and you plan to use it to improve.

4. Demonstrate good listening skills and avoid getting defensive or arguing with the person providing the feedback.

5. Keep feedback in perspective, and seek out other opinions to help you sort out the parts that seem the most true for you.

6. If you believe you have experienced discriminatory hiring practices, seek the advice of an attorney before pursuing a case, because such lawsuits can hurt your future job search.

Chapter Nine

When It's Not Working

This chapter was added after my editor-in-chief (my husband Jim) said, "What if they do everything you tell them to do, and they still never get hired?"

I said, rather indignantly, "Well, if they really follow the advice about how to prepare in *Ready for Take-Off,* and if after reading this book, they adhere to what to do and what not to do when interviewing, they are going to get hired."

He persisted, "But what if they don't? Not everyone is going to be hired."

I said, "Everyone who wants to be hired eventually is going to be hired if they follow this advice!"

Needless to say, I'm certain on this topic, because I've seen my advice work again and again. I continued, "They might not get the first job they interview for, but they will eventually get hired."

"Hmmm" he said, nodding, "Would you like a glass of wine?" My husband has secret ways to win arguments. Mostly, when he quits arguing back, he knows I'll start thinking. It's one of the benefits of having your husband be your editor. He knows how to deliver feedback. With a glass of wine.

I do know that you're going to be successful, and I care that you are successful, too. You took the time to read my book, so I encourage you to email me if you follow all of my advice, you've had multiple interviews, and you haven't been hired. It usually only takes me a little bit to guess what's been holding you back. So email me if it's not working, and maybe I can help.

However, first read this chapter. In it, I provide common reasons why it might be that you haven't been hired, despite several interviews. I want to begin with Brene Brown's definition of hope, which I think is applicable to any career pursuit. In *The Gifts of Imperfection,* Brene summarizes that "Hope is a combination of setting goals, having the tenacity and perseverance to pursue them, and believing in our own abilities." She further states, "Tolerance for disappointment, determination, and a belief in self are at the heart of hope."

It's easy to get distracted by feelings of worthlessness if you interview multiple times and don't get a job. That disappointment can be a self-fulfilling prophecy. Maintain hope. If you go into an interview thinking, *Well I probably won't get this job, either*, that belief will subconsciously transmit itself to the interview team. On the other hand, cultivating a mindset of choice will increase your hopeful feelings of getting a job.

Don't just believe in yourself as a vague concept. Believe in your ability to perform. Believe in your ability to make other choices. Believe in your ability to learn from your experiences. Most importantly believe in your ability to choose a different path or to course correct. Remember, you might not always get it right the first time.

When I decided to switch industries and move out of education, I kept my options open. I kept my mind focused on multiple choices and pathways by creating plans for all of them. I even thought it was possible I would need to take a lower-level position in order to switch industries, so that I could prove myself first.

Having spent my entire career in education, I knew that could prevent me from expanding into other types of organizations. My husband and I reworked our budget to plan for any possible outcome. It was possible I would be unemployed for a short time, or I might need to take a large pay cut.

Rather than kill my hope for the ideal position, accepting multiple possible outcomes created more hope for me. I started to be excited about learning something new. I realized I could have a lower stress level. I was excited to learn more about private industry.

When you have an enormous amount of hope, it's easier to try new methods. And it's easier to look at your job search with an expanded view. You may find that you haven't been successful quite yet because of how you're approaching the search.

Below are some possibilities to contemplate if you're not getting job offers. Only you know which ones might apply to your situation. If one possibility rings true for you, consider taking steps to alter the path on your way forward.

1. *Your expectations for the level of position you want are too high.* If you're getting interviews, but they never seem to go anywhere, this could be an indication that the level of position you list on your resume isn't comparable to what is expected at other companies. A good example of this is the position of vice president in a company. In some companies or departments a vice president role may actually be doing the duties of a lower-level director role in another company. If your interviews for other vice president roles are not successful, you might want to start interviewing for director roles.

Another way in which your expectations could be too high is because of the salary you're earning. You may have risen to a certain pay level in your current role. In order to move up in terms of responsibility, you might have to move across the lattice, not up the ladder. This is because your pay may be equal to, or more than, positions that actually have higher responsibility or greater career possibilities.

I worked with a principal in a school district that paid very well. He wanted to be a superintendent. But in order to do so, he had to take a slight pay cut when he went from a principal role in my school district to an assistant superintendent in another school district. It was worth it, however, when he eventually became a superintendent.

It feels good if your pay level increases in one organization that pays very well. But it can inhibit your ability to move to another organization and make the same amount of money. If you want to eventually move up, sometimes you need to move across in order to do so.

2. *Your expectations are too low relative to your experience.* The higher your level of experience and the higher your salary, the longer it is going to take you to find a job. Therefore, if you have to move with your spouse or you're laid off, it can seem safer to keep yourself open to lower-level positions just to keep a paycheck. Generally speaking, I agree. The problem comes when your experience is so much higher than the norm for the level of position you've applied for. In those cases, the interview team may assume you won't be happy in the lower-level position. You can combat this perception by openly addressing it in your opening or closing statement. If the team doesn't ask about it, start with, *You might be wondering why as a former vice president I am applying for director roles. Here's why I know I could bring value to the company in this director role while still challenging myself....*

3. *You're not focused enough in your job search.* If you've done a good job tailoring your resume to match job requirements, it's possible you've done so a bit *too* well. When you interview for jobs that don't exactly match your experiences, it will be apparent to the interview team when you provide your work examples. Keep in mind this can work in your favor if the team is looking for a unique perspective. It can also be a good strategy if there aren't very many candidates in that area. It's good to think broadly about your skills. You can interview with the knowledge that you have nothing to lose, and you can just be yourself,

However, if you're not getting jobs which are a stretch for you, it is probably because other candidates' experiences more closely match the job description. Highlight your skills, and if they want a traditional candidate, they simply won't choose you. If you are thoughtful about which positions you apply for at any one company, it doesn't hurt to try for positions that may be a stretch. However, keep in mind the caveat in number four, below.

4. *You're applying for too many unrelated positions at one company.* If you're doing this, you'll seem desperate. Also, interview teams will eventually catch on to what your real experiences are (or are not). Then they will quit even asking you to interview. If you are knowledgeably pursuing positions that are a stretch for your qualifications or skills, limit those applications to only one or two per company. That way, you won't look desperate.

In addition, keep in mind your time and your stamina. It takes a big effort to prepare correctly for interviews. Be cautious where you spend your time. If you spend a lot of time applying for jobs you're not really a match for, you can get weary. You don't want to be burned out by the time the "perfect match" interview comes your way. Consider if it's a better use of your time to volunteer and network. Those activities will get you more contacts than applying for multiple positions you only have a remote chance of getting.

5. *You need more connections to people who are hiring, because your job area has a very large and competitive pool of candidates.* This is one of the easiest problems to fix in theory, but it's hard for people to do. It requires getting yourself out there and actually interacting with people. There is something about going into a room full of strangers that brings all of us back to the first day of high school. Some of us panicked because we might walk into a cafeteria and find that all of our friends were assigned to first lunch, not second lunch.

Networking is not an art. It is a skill that you practice. I like to think I've gotten better at it, but I still know I can seem aloof when I get really nervous. I work on it every time I go into a new situation. Unless you have a game plan going in, these situations can create stress for you. They certainly do for me.

There are strategies that can help, however. The first strategy is to join and begin going to every professional organization meeting related to your job type. If your job area doesn't have a professional organization, volunteer for organizations where you can meet people who are hiring. Don't overlook those smaller events where you may have more time to interact with others.

Before you go to the event, write down ten starter questions you could ask anyone in the room. *Where are you from? How did you come to join this organization? Do you have kids? How long have you lived here?* If you're a real introvert, write down the questions and stick them in your pocket. Also come up with a few exit statements like, *Please excuse me, I'm going to go help doing X* or *Please excuse me, I'm going to go grab a water.*

If you get stuck, go to the bathroom and re-read your prompts. Give yourself a goal to talk to at least seven new people once. Then go back to at least three more with additional questions or dialogue. Follow this strategy and eventually you'll get to know people.

The next strategy can be even more difficult, but you can do it! Have you ever had someone you worked with ask for your help on a job search? If someone asks you to do so, you usually agree to send an email or make a phone call referral to a hiring manager. It's easy to do. It makes you feel good when someone asks for a referral or for an introduction to someone who knows the business.

You should therefore feel perfectly comfortable asking someone for a referral. Tell people you are looking for a new opportunity. Avoid approaching it as, *I need a job* and instead approach it from the perspective of, *I would love to meet for coffee or chat on the phone to gather your input regarding my job search.* In order to get your foot in the door, if you're not getting interviews or if they aren't panning out, you may need more people advocating for you. All but one job offer I've ever received came my way because I was referred. Only one was the result of a cold call application.

Another way to network is to join a temporary placement agency. These agencies place all levels of temporary positions. Their options include entry-level positions through highly skilled managerial and executive jobs. They are a great way to get to know a company and for a company to get to know you. There are some organizations that only hire from temp agencies for their entry-level jobs. This helps them have less risk because they can try out a candidate before hiring for a regular position.

6. *You're not being strategic about the type or size of companies you're applying to.* If you experienced a rough separation from your last position, you may need to be more strategic about where you apply. Some companies have professional reference checkers, extensive background reviews,

and other pathways to gather information. Using these methods, they can discover that a less-than-ideal situation occurred when you left your previous employment.

Other companies are either so large, or so small, that they don't have the time or resources to do extensive background checks. As a result, they only conduct a legal background check and verification of employment. Obviously, if you know you'll get a bad reference check from a previous employer, you should be aware what the company will find out about you when they conduct their background check.

If you have had several interviews where you became a finalist but didn't get the position, first try getting feedback. If the company gives you vague responses and doesn't give you actual feedback, your past employment troubles may have been revealed. If that is the case, quit applying at that organization. Do not make a scene to human resources about how unfair it was. Move on to another employer.

You don't want to call attention to yourself in that situation. The original hiring manager may know another hiring manager in a different organization. The information could be passed along to a second employer. If you've been applying for public sector positions, begin to focus your efforts on private companies.

It's been my experience that private companies are far more understanding of difficult job separations than are public sector employers. Perhaps this is because there are wider varieties of private company products, needs, and cultures. Hiring managers in private industries seem to have a more realistic view of employment separation reasons. They tend more to take the viewpoint that just because you're not a match for that boss/company doesn't mean you wouldn't be a match for their own.

Public sector entities are more judgmental about employment separations if there was any hint of conflict surrounding the departure. I believe this is because there are not a lot of cultural and personality differences among public employers. I also believe this is because it is usually more difficult to fire public sector workers than those in the private sector. And, most public sector workers like the security of government work, so they don't usually leave those organizations.

As a result, when hiring, public entities tend to assume that any person who didn't get along with his/her boss, or who left without a good reason, must have been a big problem. For all of the above rationale, if you haven't had success getting government jobs after becoming a finalist, I strongly recommend applying to private organizations only. If your job separation was due to a personality, political, or circumstantial conflict, those reasons are probably not going to hurt you very much in a private sector job.

If your termination was due to some sort of unethical misconduct, you should focus only on businesses or organizations you think will not do a thorough reference check. In those cases, you will also probably need to lower your expectations regarding job level and salary requirements.

7. *You're interviewing, but you're not connecting with the panel in a way that makes them like you and want to work with you.* Even if you thought you followed all of the advice in this book, it's possible that your personality is coming across as too strong/arrogant, too weak/passive or too odd/weird. It is difficult to determine if this is the case, but there are some clues you can look for.

During the interview, if the panel or interviewer always seem disinterested or bored, that may be an indication you're not connecting. When you get feedback, if it is vague, or if people constantly turn you down when you ask for feedback, those also could be indications. When the feedback is always some version of, *We just don't think your style is a match for the position* it could mean your personality is coming across as less inviting for some reason.

One way you can attempt to find out more is by asking very direct questions of the person giving you feedback. Try asking, *I was pretty nervous in the interview, and I sensed I didn't connect very well with the team. Did my personality come across as _____ or _____?* Sometimes when you ask a direct question like that, you're apt to get more specific feedback.

If you do find out that you're projecting an image not helpful to your job search, a quick fix is to get on YouTube and find all the videos you can on how to connect with an audience. Watch Amy Cuddy's TedTalk entitled "Your Body Language Shapes Who You Are" or read Amy's book entitled *Presence: Bringing Your Boldest Self to Your Biggest Challenges.* Seek candid feedback from your friends and family regarding the first impression your personality tends to make, and ask them for actionable advice about how to improve.

8. *You need more extensive assistance from an executive coach.* As a last resort, hire a career coach or other executive coach for a one-on-one interview coaching session. It can get expensive, typically $200 to $500 per hour, but if you can find someone willing to coach you for an hourly rate, it might be worth it. Executive coaches can provide a wide range of services. They are a great resource to provide perspective about your approach to the job search process. They can help you analyze what weaknesses or insecurities from the past may be hindering your ability to succeed in the interview and land the job. They can give you sample questions to answer. Then they can provide feedback regarding the tone, organization, and content of your answers. They can even provide you with

guidance regarding how your appearance is impacting others in the interview, and then give you suggestions for modifications.

In my career I constantly coach others about job search and other work-life processes. I consider myself very knowledgeable. Still, when I moved from the education industry and knew I wanted to work in the hospitality/casino world, I hired an experienced coach who works with executives at several major corporations. I wanted to get an outside perspective regarding the potential move. I wasn't entirely sure if my specific skills needed to be adapted or changed to meet private industry standards.

My coach reviewed my resume, helped guide my thinking about looking for a new job, and provided support and positive thinking when I began interviewing. She also did a follow-up session after I was on the job, just to check in and be a sounding board for my initial thinking and observations.

In summary, job searches can take time. There will be some hits and misses. However, having read this book, you are already more prepared than the majority of candidates. You have tools in your hand to help you refine your skills. If you need additional guidance, email me at stacimcintosh23@gmail.com. I can answer any quick questions you might have. If you would like more extensive help, we can arrange a one-on-one coaching session so that I can support you more fully in your job search.

Take the Shortcut

1. If you closely follow the advice I've provided in this book and my two other job search books *Job Search Passport* and *Ready for Take-Off*, I feel very confident you will receive a good job offer that meets your needs.

2. If you've had several interviews and not received a job offer, you might be making a simple mistake that is easily corrected.

3. Review the list of common issues and determine if one or more of them apply to you. If so, take the steps I've suggested to course-correct.

4. Continue getting experience and networking by attending professional meetings, volunteering, and accepting temporary positions.

5. As a last resort, you can hire an executive coach on an hourly basis to get another perspective.

Chapter Ten

Would You Like More Help?

If you would like more extensive support for your job search via phone or in person, my husband and I own a small consulting company, Sensible Solutions. Among other resources, we provide career coaching services part-time to a limited number of individuals and groups. We work for an hourly rate outside our regular work hours, which usually means early mornings, evenings, and weekends. We also have several associates we think are fabulous and will refer you to them as well in the event our schedules are unable to accommodate your specific request. Just email me at stacimcintosh23@gmail.com if you're interested.

I also have other books providing guidance for you to succeed in every aspect of your job search and career. Check out my other books on Amazon if you want to learn more details about each aspect. Every book is short, will take you about an hour to read, and is packed with practical tips you can put into place immediately. All are published as part of the *One Hour Handbook Series.*

My other books focused on job success are currently available on Amazon in the Kindle store and in paperback form:

- *Job Search Passport: Using Industry Secrets to Write Applications, Resumes, and Cover Letters*
- *Ready for Take-Off: Preparing for Interview Questions on Your Job Search Journey*
- Coming soon: *Brace for Landing: Managing Your Life and Career After Being Laid-Off, Fired, Pushed Out or Demoted*

- Coming later: *Stuck In Coach: Promotion Strategies to Land a First Class Job*

If my advice in this book helped you, please do me a favor and take a few minutes to write an Amazon book review. My commitment to readers is that I will continue to write easy to read, accessible handbooks for those who don't have the time or money to invest in expensive books, personal coaching, or on-line courses to help their career. Reader reviews help sell books, and selling books allows me the opportunity to provide more job success content to an even broader audience.

Writing a review is easy to do. If you don't want to use your real name, you can easily adapt your existing Amazon account to create an anonymous Amazon public profile name. Whatever name you choose will be on the review. Reviews let other readers like you know how the book might help them. If you take the time to write a review, I will gladly put you on my mailing list to receive free advance copies of new handbooks before they are available to the public.

Chapter Eleven

No Regrets

One of my most trusted mentors is a woman by the name of Barb Wright. Barb hired me into human resources without any experience, and she took the time to train me over ten years. At the heart of it, she is the reason I am able to write this book today. When she retired, I was hired to be Barb's replacement. Extremely wise, Barb always advised people to think, *Thank you for hiring me. Thank you for not hiring me.* The point was, if you give it your all and they still don't hire you, then you just aren't a match for that organization. Which means you wouldn't have been happy working there anyway. When you have no regrets about how you performed in the interview, it's easy to be at peace thinking to yourself, *It's their loss.*

My hope for you after your interview is that you have no regrets. I love to hear the experiences of my readers! Please share your "No Regrets" story by emailing me at stacimcintosh23@gmail.com or by posting your experience on my Facebook page @McIntoshBooks. Also feel free to email me if you have a question or if you want to give me suggestions for new content. You can also pay it forward and inspire others by sharing your "No Regrets" story as part of your Amazon book review. Experience is the best teacher, so I may use your story in future editions of this book!

Chapter Twelve

References

The additional resources referenced in this book can be found on Amazon, in e-book and paperback form, and Audible, if you prefer listening to reading. I've found that listening to informational books on my commute to work is a huge time-saver! The authors provide in-depth, additional advice on broad topics related to confidence, self-worth, and overcoming failure. I highly recommend them.

Brene Brown. *Daring Greatly: How the Courage to Be Vulnerable Transforms the Way we Live, Love, Parent, and Lead.* (New York, New York: Penguin Random House, 2012).

Brene Brown. *Rising Strong: The Reckoning. The Rumble. The Revolution.* (New York, New York: Penguin Random House, 2015).

Brene Brown. *The Gifts of Imperfection: Let Go of Who You Think You're Supposed to Be and Embrace Who You Are.* (Center City, Minnesota: Hazelden Publishing, 2010).

Amy Cuddy. *Presence: Bringing Your Boldest Self to Your Biggest Challenges.* (New York, New York: Little, Brown and Company, 2015).

Kamal Ravikant. *Love Yourself Like Your Life Depends On It.* (Kamal Ravikant, 2012).

John Maxwell. *Everyone Communicates, Few Connect.* (Duluth, Georgia: The John Maxwell Company, 2014).

Staci McIntosh can be contacted via the following:

Email: stacimcintosh23@gmail.com
Facebook: @McIntoshBooks
Twitter: @StaciVegas

I very much appreciate you taking the time to write an Amazon book review.

69096304R00064

Made in the USA
Lexington, KY
25 October 2017